Divorce with Grace

Divorce with Grace

A BOOK OF HOPE AND HEALING

by Lori Anderson

with a foreword by Dr. Joe Vitale

G R A C E

Grieve
Release
Allow the good to gush in
Create your life by design
Evolve

Copyright © 2013 by Lori Anderson & Associates

Library of Congress Cataloging-in-Publication Data

Anderson, Lori

   Divorce with Grace: A Book of Hope and Healing / Lori Anderson

ISBN: 978-1492346593

Library of Congress Control Number: 2013916393

THE HOLY BIBLE, NEW INTERNATIONAL VERSION®, NIV® Copyright © 1973, 1978, 1984, 2011 by Biblica, Inc.™ Used by permission. All rights reserved worldwide.

All rights reserved. Reproduction and distribution are forbidden. No part of this publication shall be reproduced, stored in a retrieval system, or transmitted by any other means, electronic, mechanical, photocopying, recording, or otherwise, without written permission from the publisher/author.

Dedication

To my dear brother, Todd, an Angel in Heaven
whose name I know.

Thank you for being my biggest cheerleader in life
and always believing in me.

Although I miss you immensely,
your imprint always exists in my heart and soul.

I love you forever.

Contents

- ix   Foreword by Dr. Joe Vitale
- 1   Chapter One - The Unraveling
- 15   Chapter Two - The Quest for Healing
- 33   Chapter Three - Feel it, Deal with it, Heal it
- 49   Chapter Four - Grieve
- 61   Chapter Five - Release
- 79   Chapter Six - Allowing the Good to Gush into Your Life
- 89   Chapter Seven - Create Your Life by Design
- 97   Chapter Eight - Evolve
- 109   Chapter Nine - Releasing of the Bonds: The Spiritual Divorce Ceremony
- 117   Chapter Ten - Looking Onward
- 121   Acknowledgements
- 123   About the Author

Foreword

THE OTHER SIDE OF DIVORCE

By Joe Vitale

I WAS MARRIED FOR MORE than twenty years. I loved Marian and still do, though she passed away in 2004.

Toward the end of our marriage in 1999, we realized it was time to part. She wanted to be alone. I wanted something more. We separated and began our new lives, but we stayed in touch by email and phone virtually every day, right up to the end. We remained best friends.

I think divorce has a bad rap. The media focuses on the ugly ones and prints them or airs them in the mainstream news. See enough of that and you begin to feel that divorce is just ugly, messy and hell.

If you don't think about it, you can recreate exactly what the media told you. No wonder I call what the media does *programming*. It programs you to act in a certain way. It programs you to believe divorce is awful, and life after it is horrid.

But is that true?

It doesn't have to be that way. There are loving divorces, and couples who part as friends and remain friends. I saw that a few times, and knew it was possible. So I created it in my own divorce. My ex and I remained best friends till the end.

The other thing that people fear is the idea of loneliness after divorce. Again, the media focuses on unhappy people who shoot themselves or their spouses, not on the healthy people who go on to create new lives. It's easy to think you'll be miserable and alone after divorce. Movies and TV shows tell you that.

But it isn't true.

I've gone on to meet a wonderful woman who supports me, encourages me, loves me and completes me. I believe she feels the same about me. Just last night she said she didn't have any long term goals except to spend her life with me. Very nice.

I don't know you or your situation, but I do know miracles are possible for each of us. The very fact that you are reading this book shows you to be open minded and ready for positive change. Not only can you make peace with your ex, yourself, and your situation, but you can go on to create an entirely new, exciting, loving life.

What I've learned is that our beliefs create our reality. Since what you see is colored by your perception, and your perception is created from your mindset, the central thing to do is change your mindset. That means change your beliefs.

Which beliefs?

The ones that don't serve you.

"I'll never find the right partner for me."

Does that help?

"I'm not attractive or desirable."

Does that help you?

I suggest you pay attention to your thoughts and question them. You aren't your thoughts. You have thoughts. You are separate from them. You can observe them.

The more you do it, the more you free yourself to see you can choose beliefs that empower you.

"With seven billion people on the planet, surely there's at least one good one for me." "I am beautiful just the way I am, and I'm a great catch!"

Those beliefs have power!

In short, divorce was a moment in time for you. So was high school graduation. So was your first job. Or your first kiss. Or—you name it.

Divorce isn't the end. It's the beginning.

Welcome to the next chapter of your life.
I'm excited for you!
I wonder what magic and miracles await you….

Joe Vitale
www.MrFire.com

Just when the caterpillar thought the world was over, it became a butterfly.

Proverb

Chapter One

THE UNRAVELING

Journal Entry:

Wake me up from this nightmare, this despicable nightmare where nothing makes any sense anymore. I don't recognize my husband. I feel like I'm living in the Twilight Zone. I see him standing in front of me, but when I look into his eyes, he's not there. Things just don't add up. I can't believe this is happening. Tell me this is not true. Oh where did my husband go?

How did it come to this?

How does a love so sweet turn into something so wrong? I never thought in a million years when I said, "I do," that I would now be saying, "I don't?"

Years before the divorce I had an intuitive knowing that something was wrong, but I kept trying to fight it. I wasn't going to get a divorce. That wasn't part of my plan in life. No way. I was going to be married to my high school sweetheart for happily ever after.

But I was wrong.

The day you lose trust and respect for your partner is a sad day. But that moment of clarity and truth is also a huge catalyst for healing, the beginning of a quantum leap in healing and letting go. I discovered that what I thought was true was only an illusion. I loved the feeling of certainty, certainty that my marriage with my husband would never end. That our love was strong, that nothing would ever possibly change and under no circumstance would it ever happen to us, ever. If someone would have forecasted this, I would not have believed it. I realized that this certainty I felt was only an illusion. I don't mean to say that in any hardened sort of way, but rather in an awakened awareness sort of way. Nothing is truly certain except of course, for God's love. That is certain.

If you find yourself going through a divorce or have already gone through divorce, my intention is to meet you where you are, to hold your hand, and walk you through this phase of your life over to the other side. It can be a deeply healing experience, with rewards rich and empowering on the other side. Some of our biggest learning comes when we walk through what feels like the darkest times. Someone told me once, "When you're walking through hell, don't stop to build a house. Just keep on walking." That's what we need to do in times like these.

My hope is that this book will guide you through

the healing process and expedite it so that you can get to the other side quicker with a richer, juicier life.

May you find this book a place of solace—a place to return to when you're having a tough time, a place to search for true healing and to find it, and a place to let go of the past and trust in the future.

This is an exciting, exploratory time in your life. It's time to embrace it and move forward.

Like my mother says, "Forward is the only way to go."

Grace

Grace be unto you, and peace, from God our Father, and from the Lord Jesus Christ.

1 Corinthians 1:3

My intention in writing *Divorce with Grace* is to guide you to a place where you have grace for yourself, grace for the situation, and even grace for your ex.

What does Grace mean?

Grace is about overcoming, with love. It's about seeing a negative situation and understanding that it's up to you to inject love and forgiveness, even when you know it might not change things. Grace is about acceptance, and letting go of preconceived expectations and judgments. Grace is about honor—honoring ourselves and others, by choosing to see things through a lens of love and light.

Grace is what finds us at the bottom and brushes us off and restores us, revives us.

Grace truly is about honor, and no matter what you've been through you can honor your former spouse and your situation. You can choose honor over bitterness. Honor doesn't mean you have to take abuse, expose yourself to toxic people, or give up anything. It simply means we can choose our response to a difficult situation.

You may be thinking, "Yes, but when it comes to divorce, nothing about it feels naturally graceful." And you're right, it doesn't feel graceful, unless we intentionally and consciously infuse grace into the situation. You get to deliberately choose how you are going to handle the situation, how you're going to respond, how you're going to move forward.

Whether you made the choice to end the marriage or your ex did the exiting, make the conscious choice to leave with dignity. Make a graceful exit. Take the high road. Make choices that you'll be able to feel good about when you look back over time.

Even if you feel upside down, you still have complete control over your own choices.

As you journey forward, don't lose yourself in the process. Stay strong, healthy, and surround yourself with positive, supportive people. Be mindful of the people you allow in your life, as you embark on this journey.

You're carrying a heavy load right now. There's no doubt about it. So be gentle with yourself and handle yourself with care. When a marriage dissolves, and you're left standing alone, there is a natural shakedown, and you're left staring face-to-face with what's really important in life. There's a gift in that.

You can turn this obstacle into an opportunity. You can take this lemon of a situation and turn it into the sweetest and most decadent lemonado.

You can choose to be bitter or better.

I decided for myself that I am going to be better. I am going to refine. I am going to rise to new heights. I am going to go to the edge, push past my comfort zone, and embrace my *greater yet to be*.

So I set out on a journey in search of making that happen.

When I began writing this book, the word *Grace* came to me clearly as an acronym to describe the process one travels through during the dissolution of a relationship:

G.R.A.C.E.

Grieve
Release
Allow the Good to Gush In
Create Your Life by Design
Evolve

Throughout this book, I'm going to share insights with you that I learned along the way. I'll be sharing exercises and healing techniques that will get you on the path to living your life full out, and, ultimately, seeing the light after divorce.

I want to inspire you to live your ultimate destiny and to expedite your healing process so you can get on with your amazing life. I'm here as a friend, a mentor, and a coach who's been through the process myself. Let me walk with you down this road, to a life of greater meaning and purpose.

I share my own story with you not to disparage my ex-husband but in an attempt to let you know what I've been through so you can find parallels in your own experience.

Journal Entry:
Our relationship is a complete disaster. We've

> been separated for two weeks now and have been to two "High Conflict Resolution" therapy sessions and we are even further pulled apart.
>
> In the past I've been the ROCK and have done anything and everything to work on our marriage, strengthen our marriage, save our marriage. I am now accepting that it is what it is. I'm not giving up the idea that our marriage can be saved, but I realize that ==a life with this man might not be the path for me.== God may have another plan for me and He is trying to tell me—trying to guide me.
>
> Perhaps that is why I feel like I'm banging my head up against the wall over and over again when I try repeatedly to strengthen our marriage. Always thinking that is the thing to do, the right thing to do.

There were ups and downs in my marriage, but I felt like it was a normal part of being a couple.

I had known him for two decades, and our love was a soulful, playful kind of love. We had something special. Like Romeo and Juliet, we were a perfect love story. We were connected, truly connected. When he smiled, his eyes sparkled. Or at least that's the way I saw him. My relationship with my husband was, to me, a fairy tale come true. We celebrated our joys and wins and encouraged each other continuously. When our babies were born, he was right there to deliver them, alongside the doctor. Each child went from my body into his hands and back onto my chest. He was like that. Deep, connected, soulful, and sweet. If I was the last person upstairs to the bedroom at night, I'd often find my toothbrush on the bathroom counter with the toothpaste already on it. He was just that thoughtful, and attentive to my needs.

One of the best things about us was the adventure. We were like minded that way, and both had a lust for life, love and travel. We loved to plan adventures to foreign countries, beaches, or mountains. We wanted to do it all, and I was so grateful to have a spouse that was up for anything. His mind was open.

We traveled Europe, sampling different foods, cobblestone streets, and cities. It was the first time experiencing these things and we did it together, like two kids in a sandbox. At night when we took long walks, we held hands. I appreciated him, and admired him for who he was. We talked, and spent time together. We played on a volleyball team together, had morning coffee together, and laughed, hard, all the time. Nothing was lacking. At least, that's what I thought.

Then the darkness set in. Everything changed.

It was a very strange situation. I couldn't quite figure it out. My husband was like Dr. Jekyll and Mr. Hyde. One foot in, one foot out. One day telling me how much he loved me, how amazing he thought I was, calling me his "trophy" wife, and the next telling me,

"I don't love you, I don't want to have sex with you. The perfect situation for me would be if I came home from work and you would be gone." Then back to loving on me and building me up only to come in and tear me down.

Who was this man? It was as though his whole personality changed. He told me he wanted a different life. He had five criteria. He wanted to be single, live downtown, drive a convertible, party like a rock star, and travel the world.

It was an up and down roller coaster for months, and then years. Eventually the chaos shattered my trust for him. I arrived at a place where I didn't trust him anymore. I didn't trust we'd be okay.

I was at a critical point in life, wondering what to do with my marital disaster. However, I still wasn't ready to let go. I was raised to believe that you don't get divorced. You stay married. You make it work, whatever it takes.

Years prior to my divorce, I watched an *Oprah* episode where Dr. Phil was the featured guest. His words struck a chord in my heart. They rang so true to me that I wrote them down—rewinding the recorded show over and over again until I had perfectly transcribed each word. I knew in my gut that I would need to return to this advice and read it again.

"In a marriage, particularly one with children, if you're going to get out of a marriage you have to earn your way out of that marriage. And that means you have to turn over every stone—investigate every avenue of possible rehabilitation."

He suggested going to counseling, reading books, talking to your minister—doing whatever you can do to try to make it work.

"I don't want you to be looking at your son ten years from now and him say, 'How come I had to grow up without my daddy?' And you have to say, 'Well, I don't know, we just couldn't get it together at the same time and got tired of it.' That's not much of an answer to a child who has to deal with that. If it winds up that way I want you to be able to say, 'You know what? We really had compatibility problems—let me tell you everything we did to try to preserve this and it just didn't get there.' But until you can say that, I don't think you're ready to pull the plug on this."

I was committed to doing everything I could to make it work.

We went to see a therapist several times in an

attempt to put the puzzle pieces back together, then another therapist, and another.

After meeting my husband, the therapist surmised that my husband was either on drugs, having an affair, or had a psychological condition. He said, "His behavior toward you is more than is humanly possible to take. You know it's time."

I learned through therapy that I had twisted and contorted myself into everything and anything my husband ever wanted, and nothing was ever good enough for him.

I wanted to save my marriage so badly. Relentlessly, I would do everything possible to love on it, shower it with care, heal it, and strengthen it. I loved the idea of certainty that my marriage with my husband would never end.

I still wasn't ready. I felt I needed more clarification so I sought advice from my pastor. When I met with him, he told me, "You've been fighting a nightmare for a while now and it's time to wake up." He always had interesting analogies for me. On this day he said, "After a big rainfall, when water is gushing down the street along the curb, have you ever seen a Popsicle stick that's stuck because there's a lump of debris in the way? That stuck Popsicle stick just sits and spins as the water gushes by. Eventually, water will eat wood up. ==If you stay in this marriage, it will eat you up.=="

So what do you do when the reality of the inevitable sets in?

Maybe you fall apart, maybe you crumble, maybe you get angry. I did all of those things. When the trust and comfort of a marriage comes undone you feel thrust into a firestorm of confusion. You took a vow. It was a certainty, a commitment. And now it's not there. Or, it's still there in your mind and you feel the need to fight like crazy to get it back. A divorce can feel like complete chaos. You're in pain, but you are also trying to find a solution. You're also trying to self-protect and watch your own back. It's a confusing time.

One day, I found myself driving home from the therapist's office on autopilot. I had crystal clear confirmation of what I already knew in my heart, that it was time for the marriage to end. I gripped the steering wheel and thought, "==God, I'm embarrassed that I've stayed married this long!=="

Driving along highway 360 in somewhat of a daze, I passed my exit for home and it was as though a higher force took over the wheel. It was a surreal moment. I thought, "Where am I going?" I knew I was being led.

And where did the car go? Just past the bridge and

up the hill, it turned right into the parking lot of Riverbend Church. "Oh, I see. Yes, this is where I am supposed to go." My soul, or maybe my ego, needed one more form of validation. Even though I already had countless validation through the many counselors we visited, my pastor, the friends and family who really understood the situation, and most importantly my strong gut intuition, apparently I needed yet another.

I searched for endless validation. If this sounds like you, know you're not alone.

I parked the car and just sat for a moment. The song, "If Today Was Your Last Day," by Nickelback, began to play. The words rang true to my ears.

I went inside the church, tears in my eyes, and asked to speak with one of the ministry team members. As I waited, I stood looking out the window, taking it all in.

In that moment, a memory flashed of a previous visit to the pastor when he asked, "When you look out this window, do you see the color of the trees or do you see gray?" I responded, "I definitely see color (hope)." Flash back to the present moment, standing there waiting, I certainly saw shades of gray (sadness). More than anything, though, I noticed the sunlight shining through it all.

I met with a member of the ministry team and a box of tissues in the board room. Just hearing myself talk it out loud made the validation complete. She told me how proud of me she was, how strong and courageous I was, and wished me well.

When I returned to my car, the song, "No Surprise," by Daughtry, came on the radio. Once again, the words rang true. It was no surprise that the marriage is ending—though heartbreaking, nevertheless.

Looking back I know I tried everything to make it work. If anything, I may have stayed in the marriage too long. I had reached the point of being hopelessly hopeful. But I am completely confident that the right choice was made. There are moments of sadness around the fact that our marriage couldn't survive. There are moments that my heart aches tremendously for my children when they wish for nothing more than having their parents living with them in one house, yet I have no doubt in my mind that this was the necessary result. Why? Because I did try everything I could and turned over every stone. *If you are on the fence, I strongly encourage you to turn over every stone. Keep trying. Trust that you will know when you are there.*

❖

Chapter Two

THE QUEST FOR HEALING

> Journal Entry:
> It was three o'clock in the afternoon on a sunny day when we stood in the kitchen and decided to end our marriage. He looked at me and asked, "Are we just done?" As I stood there solid and unwavering, I answered, "Yes." It was simple, brief, emotionless. As he walked away and up the stairs, I stood in the kitchen taking in the moment. "Right," I thought to myself. "This is right and complete. Thank you, thank you, thank you." Trusting the universe's perfect timing, I moved into a place of true acceptance.

WHEN HE LEFT THE KITCHEN and walked up the stairs, I felt a weight lift from my shoulders, as if we'd just laid down a corpse that we'd been schlepping around for a long time. Relief. My husband came back down moments later and we had a tactical discussion. Next steps. Sell the house, get an attorney, get the divorce papers started, and figure out finances. Our son got off the school bus ten minutes later and we were a family once again. Or at least acting like one.

Three weeks later that same, once rational, calm husband stood facing me, only this time everything we'd peacefully agreed upon seemed to disappear.

We were standing outside in the bamboo garden, and I handed him the divorce papers he'd asked me to file. He was traveling a lot and we agreed that I would take care of that initial detail. But when he read the papers, his expression turned evil. It was the standard terminology in the divorce agreement stating that neither one of us could spend over two thousand dollars during the time of dissolution. This enraged him.

"This is not going to be easy for you," he said. He began swearing at me and I followed him into the house and down the hall. "This is just the beginning," he ranted. He looked at me like a complete stranger and maliciously said, "This is about to get fun."

He got in the car and backed away and drove straight to the car dealership and bought a new convertible, even though it was a violation of the divorce decree. Several times throughout the divorce he went against the decree, so looking back with humorous hindsight, he was correct when he said this was "only the beginning." Be mindful and aware that your ex-spouse could choose to go down this road. So, be prepared.

Divorce turned my life upside down. It wasn't

something I ever imagined. And it was hard to accept that it was my reality. I didn't want the divorce. I wanted our love back. Yet once I realized that we were at the point of no return, after several counselors, books, trial separations, broken promises, I wanted nothing more than to be done with it. And move on.

During a divorce, you may feel like you are living in the Twilight Zone or a foreign land. It feels like a game of "52 Pick-Up" where someone has thrown all the cards up into the air and you're left trying to pick them all up. Scattered.

During the most difficult time of the divorce, I set out on a journey - a quest for healing, for answers. I was entangled in the pain and the memories of the life I had been living. I wanted to untangle—and to untangle in a healthy way, an expedited way, with love and grace. I had witnessed people who had been divorced, some for several years, who were still holding onto the pain...who were stuck in a rut living only half a life, and miserable as a result. I knew I didn't want that. And so the quest began.

First up, I surrendered to what was. I settled into the reality that life would be different, I would be divorced. I climbed into God's hands, nestled in and trusted that everything was going to be alright. I trusted that life would be so good, in fact, that it would be beyond my wildest imagination.

Do that. ==*Surrender to what is and trust. Know that what is happening is ultimately serving your highest good. Trust that on a deep level.*==

I read, wrote in my journal, cried, talked it out, attended self-discovery workshops and retreats, met with healers and gurus, spent time alone on the beach, and explored inward and outward ways of coping with the pain. During the roughest of times, I wrote this note to my parents who were having a difficult time accepting that divorce was the answer for anyone, but supporting me just the same:

> Mom and Dad,
>
> My heart feels so broken...the mourning can be so heavy at times that it feels like I'm mourning a death (and I guess I am—the death of my marriage, the dream of growing old with my husband and having the intact family, having a husband that was once so loving and true). Now it's just gone. It hurts so badly. Yet, it is what it is and I am moving on. I know that this is the way it needs to be. I have more peace now and my children have more peace now. And I fully believe and trust that there is another plan for me and that I am on the right path. I know that everything will turn out alright and the purpose and meaning of this divorce will all make sense someday. I know that with all my heart...it's just really tough right now. Thank you for all your caring thoughts and words, love, and support.
>
> Love you,
>
> Lori

A couple months into my divorce, I took a few days to visit my parents in Phoenix, AZ in hopes to soak up some nurturance, wisdom, and guidance as I navigated through this crazy time in my life. We took a drive up to Flagstaff to visit relatives. Along the way, we stopped in Sedona, Arizona. Sedona is known for having several healing vortexes within their red rock mountains. This intrigued me, so of course I had to check it out. We stopped at a souvenir shop and got a map for the vortexes. My parents didn't think much about all this energy business so they dropped me off at the base of the rock while they went on their merry way to get lunch at McDonald's.

Nothing felt like it could feed me more than the quiet solitude in this natural wonder.

I followed my map and hiked up to the vortex area. When I reached the plateau, the scene opened up to a beautiful vista that went on and on for miles. I stood on the plateau, overlooking the vista of my life, trying to find the meaning of it all.

I found the perfect spot. I sat down at the overlook of the energy vortex where the juniper trees grow twisted by all the immense energy. I felt rooted and grounded on the red rock. I noticed a fascinating woman—a beautiful woman standing at the top of the rock, wearing a white dress, with her hair flowing in the breeze. She looked like a woman of wisdom, an angel, actually. I was drawn to her so I walked toward her and we met.

There was an immediate connection, and in our conversation we could see ourselves in one other. In other words, our stories, the things we were going through, were similar. We each had stories of our long loves that were now leaving. We were both at a transitional time looking at our lives, wondering, "What are we going to do with our lives?" She was wondering where she should move—should she move back to England or California? She was in Sedona to try to gain some clarity and figure it out.

I was in the same dilemma, move to California as our intact family had been planning to do or do I stay in Austin? What do I do? What is the best scenario? She was an energy healer and she said to me, "You know what? We are the ones who gave our power away. It's our responsibility because we gave it away. And now in our growth and evolution through this process, it's important that we know our power and that we keep our power."

There was an immeasurable feeling of calm, warmth, and love now sitting right in the vortex. Clarity. Feeling the love of Mother Earth. A warm hug of loving energy.

Linda, the beautiful healer woman that I met at the top of the vortex, held my hands and said to me,

"Before you know it, your life will be so beautiful! This is a happy time!" And I thought, "I know, I know." Just then the sun popped out and everything became more vivid and more beautiful.

We gave each other a hug and fully enjoyed our brief but soulful encounter. I have no idea where she is or what her last name is but she is a woman I will never forget. I believe that there are no accidents in those whom we meet. We shared love and good wishes for one another.

Before you know it, YOUR life will be so beautiful.

In your releasing process, along your journey, make sure to pay attention to God's messengers. People will come into your life for a reason. They speak truth into your situation, and it can help change your path.

Linda had said, "The truth is, we gave our power away," and in many ways I know that to be true. I had given up so much. And yet, I had been willing to give up even more to be with him. Her words were profound, and at that moment, exactly what I needed.

There are no accidents. The encounter with Linda was a turning point in my life. It helped me transform. It helped me see things in a different way.

Think about the messengers you've encountered.

One day I arrived home to find that my ex had been

in the house. The house we once shared. Regardless of what the courts had said, throughout our divorce, he ignored it and did what he wanted. I felt violated. I was distraught, protective of my home, and I was pacing up and down the halls and through the living room, angry. "Who does he think he is?" Just then, the doorbell rang.

I looked out the peep window of the wooden Tuscan door, saw two young men and knowing full well what this was about thought, "Good Lord!"

I flung it open with a weary look on my face. "Yes?"

The two men standing there could see the wild look in my eyes. It was obvious that something was wrong. I couldn't hide it.

"Hello, ma'am?"

They were wearing black pants and white shirts. They held Bibles. They both smiled, peacefully.

Their insides did not match mine. I was not feeling peaceful.

"Can we help you with anything?" one asked.

I ranted and raved a bit while my boys were running around uproariously in the background, then as gently as I could explained that I didn't have time to visit right now, and *assured* them that I love Jesus. They asked if they could help me move furniture, or help me do something around the house. "Is there anything we can do?"

"No, not unless you've got a miracle in that bag of yours." I said, with a deep sense of honesty and a slight dash of sarcasm.

In humorous hindsight, those two young men probably didn't know what in the world to make of me.

They handed me a picture of Jesus, smiled, and left. They had written a phone number on the back of the picture and assured me that I could call it anytime, day or night.

I put the picture of Jesus on my vanity mirror. Shortly afterwards, my girlfriend, Michele, came over. As I told her the story, she couldn't help but laugh. Then she said, "Listen, if you need someone to talk to, you call me before you call that number."

It was a moment that reminded me that no matter how crazy things get, you can laugh about them later.

Receiving that picture of Jesus was a moment of grace.

On my vanity, next to my picture of Jesus, I created a shrine of positivity. There I placed a small rock with the word *Believe* on it, a plaster heart that my oldest son had made and painted red with gold glitter sprinkled on top of it, a butterfly made with blue tissue paper by my youngest son, the Serenity prayer, and cards with positive affirmations written on them.

I also took a white board marker and wrote at the top of my mirror:

> *"For I know the plans I have for you," declares the Lord, "plans to prosper you and not to harm you, plans to give you hope and a future." (Jeremiah 29:11)*

Seeing this shrine of positivity brought the feeling of peace to my heart and hope to my spirit. It also reminded me of the healing and transformation that was naturally taking place.

During this time in your life, it's very important to take time for yourself. Pull yourself out of your normal environment. Spend time in nature. Whether you go on an exotic trip, a simple hike just down the road, a drive to the lake, or a walk on the beach, it's grounding and nurturing to still yourself in nature. It can bring you peace.

I went to a Spiritual Women's Retreat at the Balcones Retreat Center in the Texas hill country. Little did I know when I signed up for the women's weekend through my church that the retreat was titled, *Journey On*. "How perfect," I thought. We stayed in little cabins nestled in the woods, four women assigned to each one. It was like summer camp all over again. I loved it. Four creaky little cots and a desk. Four soulful women and a mission to journey on. I felt like I was surrounded by an abundance of love and hope. We settled into camp with a welcome dinner at the pavilion and an evening hike out to open grounds for a roaring bonfire, beautiful music, and s'mores.

The next morning, we enjoyed sunrise pilates, and a short hike to a perfect little spot among nature for fellowship. One of my roommates, Judy, led the scripture.

> *"So humble yourselves under the mighty power of God, and at the right time he will lift you up in honor. Give all your worries and cares to God, for he cares about you (1 Peter 5:6-7)."*

That night we had communion under the stars. It was beautiful. I cried deep sobs. I cried out to God for peace and healing.

Tears are part of healing grace. I could feel the healing happening.

The next day, we had the opportunity to participate in the adventure of zip lining from one end of the lake to the other. I got myself harnessed up and climbed to the take-off perch. As I zipped across the lake, practicing my own version of aerial ballet, I screamed with absolute delight. Oprah says that when you're going through a tough time, just keep in mind, "The 'wee' moment is coming!" *Trust that things are about to change for the better.* I felt my first 'wee' moment as I sailed through the air above Lake Ted.

As I was packing up my Jeep and getting ready to head back home, Judy came running over to me. "I have something for you," she said. It was a 2×2 inch card, light blue in color. "I have several of these on a silver ring in my car and I felt inspired to give you this particular one." On one side, it said, "Do not be afraid, stand firm and you will see the deliverance the Lord will bring you today (Exodus 14:13)," and on the other, "When you pass through the waters, I will be with you; and when you pass through the rivers, they will not sweep over you (Isaiah 43:2)."

I propped it up on the console in my car and it's been there ever since. Every time I look at it, I smile and feel comfort.

I was making progress in healing but I couldn't shake this relentless feeling of failure. When divorcing, you can feel like a total failure. So how do you deal with failure—the sense of failure after a divorce?

For me it was a quest for healing and trying to let go of that. I was seeking the answer, for resolution in my mind. The moment that it happened for me was when I was in the spiritual city of Fairfield, Iowa, sitting at a dinner table in a little Asian restaurant with a wise man who was talking to me about this very topic. It was some of the worst Asian cuisine I had ever had but the conversation was so rich that it didn't much matter.

I shared with him that despite the fact that I've accepted the divorce and have even embraced it, there's a piece of me that feels a deep sense of failure.

He said, "You did not fail. You did not fail at all. You are not the failure. The marriage failed. You are you. The failed marriage, it does not define who you are. You are not the divorce. Don't allow yourself to get lost in that experience and overshadowed by it. If you lose yourself, if you so identify with the experience, you can forget your true nature…which is unbounded and happiness and consciousness."

At that moment it clicked with me. *You did not fail. The marriage failed.* It made sense to me, and I was able to release the guilt and burden and the sense of failure that comes with the ending of the marriage.

While going through divorce, be sure to nurture and nourish yourself.

Take the time it takes to grieve and to heal. It is important that you give yourself comfort, solitude, and time with God to be comforted. Be okay in your aloneness. How many times have you had the chance to be alone?

Make sure you give yourself the gift of taking time to read inspirational works. Or plunge into an Oprah Soul series online. Surround yourself with positivity. Be mindful, and take care of yourself. Turn to God and pray. And also take time to do nothing but sit. My writing coach taught me this very valuable lesson. It's called "taking time for the park bench" where you go to a park and you just sit with no agenda, no cell phone, nothing. Truly yourself. Enjoy the moment of the park bench—just observing and "being."

~

During the worst of times, the very best thing I could've done was to give myself the gift of comfort.

Seek in your mind ways that you know will provide you comfort. You know what comforts you better than anyone else. Take a moment now to make a list as a go-to page of comfort. There are times when we are feeling frazzled and we are feeling scared and we are feeling hurt and totally stressed out and overwhelmed. That is the time to turn to this list because when we are frazzled we don't always think about the things that really give us comfort and joy.

Create your list now of what's true to you, what brings you those comforts. Refer to it anytime you need it to bring you back to center and to your true groundedness. In a frazzled moment, that list can be your saving grace. It was for me.

Here are some examples: taking a warm bubble bath surrounded by candles, taking time to meditate and connect to God, go on a hike in nature, spend time at the beach, wrap yourself up in a warm blanket with a cup of hot tea. Go have the most kick-ass workout you've ever had, or dare yourself to run so hard until you feel like you're ready to collapse. What fits your personality? Start making a list, today.

Exercise:

In the space on the next page, make a list of ten things that comfort you. Think of it as a survival kit that you go to when you're in chaos. It might be something simple, like going to the bookstore, or having a hot bath. It might be a massage, or a workout, a trail run, or a good book.

1. _____

2. _____

3. _____

4. _____

5. _____

6. _____

7. _____

8. _____

9. _____

10. _____

I recommend keeping a copy of this list in your wallet or on your phone. Reference it when you're having a panic moment, or a crisis.

While this is a great list to refer to, I want you to take it a step further. Now that your list is complete, turn to your calendar and deliberately schedule at least one of these items per week for the next 12 weeks. Do this for you. Nurture yourself. This list you've created is a great gift for yourself. It's a tool that I want you to honor and use wisely, not only as a reactionary strategy when you're stressed and feeling frazzled but also as a proactive tool to keep yourself grounded and centered.

Healing is different for everyone. It might take months for one person to heal. But for another it could be a shorter period. No matter which camp you fall into, it's important to feel it and deal with it so you can heal it. So many times people will plunge into their work, or their addiction, instead of facing the pain. But it's important to look in the mirror and face it.

❈

Chapter Three

FEEL IT, DEAL WITH IT, HEAL IT

*Tools to take with you along the Journey:
Cultivate Awareness, Be an Observer,
The Power of Journaling*

Journal Entry:
In my greatest despair as I was going through the divorce, a friend looked me in the eyes and said, "You're not only going to survive, you're going to thrive!"

I HELD ONTO THOSE WORDS, especially when times got tough, and I want you to hold on to those words as well.

You're not only going to survive, you're going to THRIVE!

Your new beginning is going to be exciting. But first you must deal with the "now" and deal with it fully so that your next chapter in life, your 'greater yet to be,' can be truly great, without any residue fogging up your future.

What does healing mean? The word healing is derived from the root word, whole. It's the sense of returning to wholeness. It's the feeling that 'all is well' again.

Wouldn't it be great if we could fast forward past the grieving part of the divorce? Many people have attempted that. Some delve into excessive partying. Some dive deeply into their work. Some run right into the arms of another, believing this is the answer. But doing so could be detrimental. You must feel and deal with the pain so you can heal it. In order to move on with your life and become whole, it is essential that you go into the pain.

Divorce and all that comes with it can generate a pain like no other. It feels as though the pain and devastation inhabits every cell of your being. The "sting of the nose" feeling as the tears began to well up radiates down to the "socked in the stomach" sensation. If you feel like you've been betrayed, you may feel like a knife has been stuck into your back. For me it felt like the knife went all the way through, from my back into my body and out the front. And the physical pain was real.

You may recall every moment that led to the demise of the marriage. You may be flooded with questions, all the "what ifs" and "if onlys". You may find your heart and mind are playing tug of war at times.

The pain of divorce can be excruciating. Crushing. Sometimes you feel like you can barely breathe. Love is a strong emotion and it's being ripped apart. Your commitment is being ripped apart. Everything you trusted and believed in, ripped apart.

When going through divorce, you may experience a whole plethora of emotions. You may feel heartbroken. You may feel disbelief. You may feel lonely, scared, sad, abandoned. People have described this experience in the following ways:

I feel lost.
I feel like I'm floundering.
I feel like there's a fog over my life.
I feel like a leaf blowing in the wind.
I feel like I've lost my identity.
I feel like I've checked out.
I feel like a total failure.

At a workshop I facilitated, one of the participants shared her experience with divorce, "Nothing has ever hurt this much," she said. "It hurts my soul. I'm sad. I'm tired. He's the person who's never supposed to hurt me like this. We had an agreement that we'd be together forever. There's no back door."

Another woman shared that after many years of being divorced, she hadn't completely healed yet. "I haven't resolved the pain and I carried it into my next marriage. I did it all wrong. I never went off to be by myself. I never had time to be independent. I went from one relationship and literally moved into the house of another. I never had time for me. I think I never healed. It's twelve years later and I still cry about my divorce. Questioning my choices. I wish I had done things differently. I wish I had taken time for me. Time to heal. Time to get to know me. I still yearn to do that. I need to do that."

This is why it is essential that you delve into healing now. Plunge into the thick of the pain while it's fresh. Deal with it now, even when it's uncomfortable. Be cognizant not to shove the feelings under the proverbial rug, only to find them come back and hit you with a vengeance later, disrupting your life all over again.

Let it out. Write it out. Talk it out. Cry it out. Dance it out. Pray. Repeat.

Healing takes the time it takes. It might take months for one person to heal. For another it could happen faster. Be gentle with yourself. I repeat, be gentle with yourself. It is a process. At times, you may find yourself feeling completely liberated, like, "I got this!" Other times, you may find yourself on the floor crying, or feeling like you could collapse to the floor in an instant. The feelings can be incredibly intense and they are real. Whatever you are feeling, allow yourself to fully feel it. Go into the pain. And when it's joy you're feeling, fully go into the joy and be grateful for it. This is the process of true healing—you must first feel it, then deal with it, so that you can heal it.

Tools to Take with You on the Journey

I recommend three powerful tools to take with you on your journey toward healing. Cultivate Awareness, Be an Observer, and The Power of Journaling. You can utilize these tools continuously as you go through each step of the G.R.A.C.E. process—Grieve, Release, Allow the Good to Gush into Your Life, Create Your life by Design, Evolve.

Cultivate Awareness

Your body is a complex engine of mind, body, and soul, with thousands of emotional sensory experiences, feelings, smells, sights and sounds occurring in any given day. Right now, it might be battered and bruised. You may have experienced emotional stress, distraction, anger, or rage. Your work life may have been interrupted, as you found it difficult to concentrate. Fear and anxiety may have crept in. Now is the time to bring yourself back to center, and become hyperaware of everything going on inside. Being aware of your emotions will help you navigate them.

Although life can feel like it's over, it's not over. It feels that way because this phase of your life is over. The truth of the matter is life as you know it is over. Let me repeat, life as you know it is over. That's it. Not to minimize the situation because it is huge. However, in the bigger picture of life when you look back it's not going to have the power and magnitude that it has now. It will just be a piece of your life. A fragment. Just like when you reflect on something that was highly relevant in your life ten or twenty years ago—even two years ago—and it's not anymore. Holding this perspective can help in the healing process by helping you to see that regardless of how heavy this is, it's simply a phase, a blip on the radar screen, in terms of the 'whole' of life. A phase. And this too shall pass.

I was visiting Mindy Audlin's positive and uplifting "What If Up?" group at Unity Church. When I shared my story, a few people who had been through divorce themselves years prior looked at me with complete understanding and said, "The next year is going to be crazy. Divorce is a crazy time." Just hearing that, knowing that, and keeping that in the back of my mind was helpful. Keep this as a baseline thought. When things feel crazy just remember, "Yeah, that's normal and it's getting better every day." Each passing day is a day closer to the return of the good times.

When your life is in upheaval it's hard to gauge whether or not you're thinking clearly. It may not be a good time to make important decisions. Create space for awareness, and be in tune with your entire holistic self. Body, mind, emotions, and spirituality. Don't always act on your emotions. Stop, wait, listen, and think.

Know that the feelings that you have faced or are experiencing now are temporary. See the emotion. Use your intellect to see it as an emotion that you are simply experiencing, knowing that it is temporary and knowing that it will pass. With the power of our minds we can shift the way we feel.

First really feel the sadness—for healing's sake—but make the choice to move out of that feeling and not linger there too long or to get stuck in it. So now, again from an intellectual standpoint of recognizing that this is simply an emotion that is being experienced, you can look at it square in the face and say, "Thank you for visiting. Thank you for helping me feel the emotion to heal this pain. You may leave now."

Give yourself permission to free yourself allowing the sadness not to linger for too long. Then make a shift. Cognitively shift to doing something positive - listen to uplifting music, spend time in nature, meet up with a friend, or write a gratitude list. Do something that brings you comfort, that's nurturing and makes you feel great.

For example, people often find comfort in things like:

- Music
- Dancing
- Writing
- Running
- Hiking
- Meditating
- Watching comedy
- Listening to inspirational CDs

You may want to add these to the comfort list we talked about in Chapter 2, to have as a prepared go-to reference when you want to shift out of a negative feeling space—because when we're feeling down, sometimes it's hard to think of these things.

If you haven't made your list yet, please pause and make it now.

Be an Observer

When you can see your life from the outside, the road to healing becomes clearer. But it takes work. You've got to look outside of yourself, and step out of your grief or wherever you happen to be, and have faith in the unknown.

It's helpful to pull yourself out and look at your life

as the observer, as God sees you. This divorce is just something that's happening in your life. It's a phase. It's the divorce phase. Pull yourself out and look at it from a distance, as a time in your life that you're just passing through. Divorce is just passing through this phase of your life. It's as if you could say, "Well, hello, divorce. I see you and you're happening." Soon you'll be able to say or maybe you can already say, "Goodbye divorce. I'm done with that, it's complete."

Trust and know…that the divorce, this occurrence that happened in your life, this experience, has come to serve you. It has served your highest good in some form or fashion. Recognize that. See that as a gift that has happened in your life.

What has happened? What are the gifts? Are you a stronger person today than you were? Or maybe you're going through the toughest part of the divorce where you feel there's no strength left at all. But trust and know that you will have more strength. You will be stronger as a result of this happening in your life. And then in the future, in some way, you'll be able to light the path and help others go through this phase of their life.

Old feelings may come back up from time to time, even though you've moved on and you feel healed. You may move from sadness, to joy and then experience another wave of despair. Recognize these are just feelings. Observe. They don't own you. You own the feelings.

Part of any successful journey is cultivating awareness about your own path, and emotional triggers. Do you know when you're starting to slide into sadness, or depression? Are you aware of what sets you off, makes you feel bad, or takes you back to the negative memories? Everyone has peaks and valleys, and being aware of how you handle each phase of your life is an important part of thriving.

Sometimes people don't see or understand their triggers unless they're self-aware. Try to notice what triggers sadness in you. A song? A movie? Many people who have traveled through divorce shared that it was the "divorce firsts" that were the hardest—the first wedding anniversary, the first birthday alone, their children's birthdays, Christmas, Valentine's Day, family vacation, etc.

A trigger can send you into a dark hole of sadness—if you don't understand it's only a trigger of emotion. Recognize your triggers, feel them, and realize they are only emotions passing through. Remember the emotion doesn't own you. Make the choice to cognitively shift your mind, and move on.

You can also be proactive when you know that a special day or event that could be a trigger is about to occur. I remember when the first post-divorce passing of my wedding anniversary was about to occur. I wasn't sure how I'd feel so I proactively scheduled a massage and planned a play date for my boys to be at my best friend's house with her three boys. It felt so good to pamper myself; to give myself a gift. It didn't hurt that I scheduled it with a sensual, Uruguayan massage therapist either. But I digress.

After the soulful and nurturing massage, I stopped at the grocery store to pick up some ice cream and cones for all the kiddos. Knowing what they liked, I picked out a gallon of half chocolate half vanilla. As I waited in line at the checkout counter, I realized it was the exact time of our wedding ceremony. I looked down and noticed the name of the ice cream: The Great Divide. Then I looked up with a giant smile and thought "God, you have such a sense of humor!"

If you come across a trigger, observe it and don't allow it to overtake you and get you to a place where you're feeling stuck. It is not you. It is not your life. It is not your story. It's just a feeling, so experience it as that. Having this perspective changes the way you understand and experience it, the way you look at it. It allows you to move on with your life with more ease and bliss and joy knowing that it's part of the human experience to feel like this from time to time.

See the sadness as a visitor, allowing it and accepting it and letting it go.

One difficult truth about divorce is that you can't control the other person's actions. So if they ignite a spark of anger, have an emotional outburst, or if they start a fight or intentionally disrupt your life, you may be forced to respond. Although you may have passed through a releasing stage into grace, it might feel as if you are being pulled back into a tidal wave of emotions again. This is an especially effective time to be aware of your triggers by being an observer. Stopping and observing will help you make smarter choices and take the higher road.

The Power of Journaling

There is great healing power in journaling. Sitting down, opening a book and simply writing out your thoughts and feelings. So many thoughts swirl through your mind. They have to go somewhere or they'll just keep swirling and that can feel crazy-making. A journal is a great place to set it free. Writing down your thoughts and feelings helps make sense of things, puts order to your thoughts. There's also great benefit and reward when at a later time, you look back over your journal writings and you can see just how far you've come along.

I am grateful that I began journaling early on and that I captured many thoughts and emotions that I'm able to look over now. Journaling is profoundly healing. When you write down your innermost thoughts it's a release, and a positive flow of energy. The thoughts, emotions, and "junk" that was stored up inside you is now out, on the table. Sometimes it's freeing to look back over what you wrote to see how far you've come. At other times it's better to toss the letters, journals, or pages into a fire in an act of finality and release. Or, it's possible that you'll just journal and then never look at them again. Regardless of what happens with your words I encourage you to write. As you travel on this journey, write down your feelings and emotions as you feel led. Get it out.

Exercise:

In this exercise, the goal is to write continuously for 15 minutes. You can choose one of the writing prompts below to get you started (or use one of your own):

I feel…
I'm frustrated…
What's going on in my life is…
The thing that hurts the most is…
What I want is…

If you find times when you're struggling, acknowledge it and write it down. Journaling is a great way to express yourself and find discoveries that help resolve personal issues.

Keep in mind that the divorce may never seem to make complete sense to you. Some things just can't be figured out and understood, as the great poet, Rainer Maria Rilke, suggests:

I beg you....to have patience with everything unresolved in your heart and try to love the questions themselves as if they were locked rooms or books written in a very foreign language. Don't search for the answers, which could not be given to you now, because you would not be able to live them. And the point is to live everything. Live the questions now. Perhaps then, someday far in the future, you will gradually, without even noticing it, live your way into the answer.

Even if you got to a point where you felt it all made sense as to why the marriage fell apart, even then it may not be accurate. It's merely your perception of the "why's" and the "what's." It's important not to get hung up on the idea that you have to make sense of it all before you can let go of it, to forgive the situation, and to move on with your life. If you choose to hold on and be rigid about needing to figure it all out before you can move on, you may be stuck for a long time. What good can that do for you?

When I learned this, I felt a true freedom come over my mind. The play and replay in my mind of so many scenarios of my marriage just stopped. There's real value in taking the time to reflect on what happened, to learn and grow and become a better you, but stop pressing the replay button and let go.

Chapter Four

GRIEVE

Journal Entry:
I woke up this morning feeling devastated. Even though I've accepted the divorce, I'm sad that our marriage couldn't be turned around and be loving and joyful again. It hurts deeply. It's the first thing I think about when I wake up and the last thing I think about before falling asleep.

How DOES ONE ENCAPSULATE the pain that is felt, experienced, breathed, when divorcing? That intensely strong pain that is palpable—seemingly felt in every cell of the body. Are there words that fully describe the depth and breadth, the embodiment of this particular pain? Probably not, at least not to the magnitude that it's felt. And if there are, those words and descriptions are deeply personalized to each individual going through this transition.

In writing this book, it became clear to me that releasing and grieving doesn't mean the same thing for everyone. I've encountered some people who handled divorce with minimal emotional pain and others who felt extreme grief. You learn a lot about yourself throughout the process and grieving is a part of it. But grieving doesn't have to mean that you experience complete emotional upheaval. Sometimes grieving is more about letting go, or seeing things in a new light, or restoration, or gratitude.

In this chapter I'll talk about the first word in the acronym G.R.A.C.E.—grieving.

Grieving, Glorious Grieving

Just when the caterpillar thought the world was over, it became a butterfly.

Proverb

According to Elisabeth Kübler-Ross, there are five stages of grief: denial, anger, bargaining, depression, and acceptance. With the death of a marriage, the mourning process can go into full effect. To go through each of these stages is completely normal. It is also normal to swing in and out of each of these stages. You may grieve, release, and then grieve again. It's tempting to feel as if you'll experience each emotion in a certain order or stage, but the reality is you might experience many emotions at once, or many stages more than just once.

Grieving and healing go hand in hand. They're intermingled. When you pass through grief, remember that healing is on the other side. Healing is a process. Healing doesn't happen all at once. It happens in increments.

It all begins by acknowledging your grief.

There is a time to mourn. There is a time to laugh. You will laugh again. Take the time to mourn now while you need it.

Perhaps you've passed through some (or all) of the stages of grieving. Below, an example is provided for each stage.

Denial

Shortly after my own journey through divorce, a beautiful woman in her 50s walked into my workshop. She looked like her spirit had been hit by a Mack truck. I could tell it took all she had to pull herself together to get to the workshop. She was proper and poised, and wore a twin cardigan and pink dangling earrings to complete the look. She had a sweet essence about her, of a good heart and soft, yet frail soul.

She was distraught, and with good reason. She shared with the group that her high school sweetheart, beloved husband of 30+ years, and father of her only son, had made an announcement to her on Christmas Eve, "I'm in love with another woman and starting a new life with her," he said. "Oh, and that second house we just bought in San Diego to spend half the year where our son lives is actually where she and I will be living."

Well, Merry Christmas!

A million thoughts flooded her mind—disbelief. "This can't be happening!"

She was convinced that this was just a phase and that they'd get back together when he came to his senses. Their whole life had been planned out. Their plan had consisted of them spending the rest of their lives together. Her husband had just retired so their well-thought-out and fun plan was supposed to be just beginning.

Unfortunately there are thousands of stories that resemble that one. No matter what you are going through, you are not alone. I've met countless people who are in the shock and disbelief stage of a divorce. You may feel like you've checked out, but you will check back in.

Anger

Some get angry for a short time where others feel anger throughout their entire divorce process. Every individual is different. You'll react and feel differently than someone else might, yet we all experience commonalities. It's common to feel abandoned, rejected, angry, and sad. It's common to desire revenge or feel confusion. And it's common for people to want to cover up any pain with other things in order to numb it.

I remember a time when I was extremely angry over my ex's malicious intentions and desiring a constructive outlet for that anger (so that I wouldn't rip my ex's head off or allow my own to implode from all the stress). Anger is a strong emotion—a force to be reckoned with. It's very normal and healthy to feel anger when going through the experience of divorce. What's important is that we deal with the emotion in a healthy way. I found myself drawn to the idea of martial arts. I signed my two boys and myself up for a series of classes to enjoy as a family bonding experience, to put our focus on something new, and to let out any frustrations we may be carrying.

Before the family classes started, the instructor suggested that I come in for a private session. So when my boys were off to school, I walked into the martial arts studio for my one-on-one self-defense training session with the Master of Martial Arts.

After teaching me some basic upper and lower body defense moves, we focused on kicks. Once I had the kicks down, he challenged me to kick him across the room. He held a sparring pad and instructed me to kick him so hard that he would be forced to take a step back. We started at one end of the room. Each time I kicked him hard enough he'd step back but if I didn't give it my all, he would take a step forward, making it take longer to get across the room and claim victory.

So we began. I kicked hard and it felt awesome. I felt strong. I kicked again. He yelled, "Use your power! Let out your frustration!" With each kick, I screamed the thoughts inside my head, "How could you be so careless with our family? How could you be so reckless with my heart? You selfish prick!"

He pressed hard and I got pushed backwards. He demanded more from me. "Kick harder! Use your power!" I kicked harder. I wobbled for a second. It was intense. I re-focused and kicked harder yet. My heart had never pounded that hard. There was such a strong surge of emotions and adrenaline pumping through my body. I realized I wasn't even half way across the room yet. I was sweating profusely and my body was aching. I had thought this challenge was going to be easy. It was hard, but there was no way I was stopping. I listened to his words, "Use your power!"

At the end, I bent over in exhaustion. My heart was racing and I could barely catch my breath. Toward the end of the challenge, I felt like I could've died. But I didn't. I made it to the other side.

This exercise was a powerful and constructive challenge that turned out to be a great metaphor for the process of divorce. There are times when you feel powerful and there are times when you feel like you're dying. But you'll make it to the other side, victoriously.

Allow yourself to really feel the anger, in a healthy constructive way. Let it out.

Bargain

When the harsh reality of divorce begins to set in, it's not uncommon to find yourself negotiating in your mind or with your ex. You may decide perhaps 'if I change this or he stops doing that' we could save our marriage after all.

There are many unknowns about the future at the time of a divorce. With this uncertainty, you may be asking yourself, "Is divorce what I truly want? Can I do it on my own? Will my kids be ok? Will I ever find love again? Will I end up alone?" These uncertainties can sometimes seem worse than an unhappy or unhealthy relationship.

Bargaining seems to walk a fine line with denial. It can set up a false premise that the marriage could be alright. Bargaining rarely provides a sustainable solution.

In my own marriage, during the separation phase, my husband and I decided that we didn't want a divorce, we wanted our love back. We began a natural process of bargaining - searching for ways in which our marriage could survive. I absolutely hated being apart from my children when it was Dad's weekend. That missing feeling in my heart was excruciatingly painful. I thought if I reconciled, I'd get to be with my kids all the time.

When I told one of our dear friends from college who's a lawyer that we were planning on reconciling, he said, "Listen, you both tried this before and you failed, so I think you need to write up a contract with one another. Put it on paper. Show that you're committing to doing these things because you value your marriage so much." And so we did. We went to the extreme of writing up a contract and both signing it. With our "solid" plan in place, I called the attorney and put a stop to the divorce.

We reconciled and moved back in together. We were happy and grateful that we were able to save our marriage. About a year later, the promises began to unravel again. By the following year, it was clearly over.

What made me believe it would work that time? Especially since they were agreements we had tried once before? Fear perhaps? An inordinate amount of hope? The desire to feel deeply loved again?

Have you found yourself bargaining during your own divorce process? Are you still bargaining?

Depression

Typically, there comes a deep sadness with the ending of a marriage, whether you wanted the divorce or not. Feeling sadness is a sign that you've moved beyond denial and have begun to accept the situation.

I remember the sadness was heavy and tormenting. I never thought I'd be divorced. I was forced into a paradigm shift. I missed him—the good parts of him. I missed having my family all together in one home. I remember the first night that my kids were off spending the night with their dad, how odd and sad it felt as I passed their bedroom at bedtime. It felt like they were ripped away from my heart. I thought, "This isn't right. This isn't how it's supposed to be." My heart ached for them. I wished things had turned out differently. Even though I knew in my heart that this is how life needs to be now and that this was healthiest for my kids and me, it still hurt like crazy.

Grieving over a divorce is really all about saying goodbye to all things familiar. Waking up with your spouse, seeing your kids every day, having the family together on Christmas morning, and perhaps close ties you once had with your ex's family.

When I was feeling sad I would imagine myself surrounded by a cocoon of God's love and protection. Try it. *Sink into the feeling of a warm embrace of God's grace.* Notice how your body just relaxed. Shoulders perhaps dropped down, muscles softened, and a feeling of being more at ease comes over you.

Acceptance

One night I was reading, *Too Good to Leave, Too Bad to Stay*, a book given to me by my friend, Belinda, which coincidently I had paged through at Barnes & Noble one night about seven years prior. Reading it now with fresh eyes, it sparked an analogy in my mind that helped me see more clearly and get past getting "overly" hung up on the good attributes of my husband.

Imagine you're living in a beautiful house with amazingly gorgeous windows and stunning hardwood floors, and an incredible, breathtaking view. You love this house. You're grateful for this house. You see yourself spending the rest of your life in this house. You see yourself decades from now sitting on the swing with your grandkids. You feel joy!

Then you find out that there's a huge crack in the foundation and the house is not sitting on stable ground. You're devastated. The contractor says this is repairable. What a relief! Yes, there's hope…even though this is a mess and will cost a lot of money and upheaval moving out temporarily. With time and patience, there is hope.

After the repair you learn the foundation is still unsteady. New fractures are showing up. There's so much pressure. Despite the best of efforts, they can't be stopped. They're spreading. Pieces of the foundation are crumbling. No amount of love and appreciation for the gorgeous windows or the hardwoods will change the fact that the house is no longer safe. It's not sustainable, despite how badly you want it to be.

So now it's time to take action, to make a choice. Move out and get your most precious things out safely and start again, or stay in the house for as long as possible and likely being stuck in it when it collapses and see your most precious belongings destroyed, yourself included.

It may sound somewhat frivolous to compare a marriage to a house, but if your house was in that condition, would you "accept" the need to move? Would you move on?

As my friend Barbara told me, "Sometimes it's hard to see the whole picture when you're stuck inside the picture frame."

Remember, healing takes what it takes. Be gentle with yourself. Allow yourself to experience your grief. *Love yourself forward.*

It might be hard to imagine now but things will get better. They will. You'll see.

Your pain will pass. It will eventually fade to a distant memory.

As you begin the releasing process in the next chapter, you will find that the load you are carrying will begin to lighten up.

Chapter Five

RELEASE

Journal Entry:

Today I became divorced. I became single. And I became "officially" Lori Anderson! Wow. What a relief to be completely done with this process, this chapter. There was so much energy and mental toughness and emotional feelings throughout the last 10 months (and much more) that it feels exhilarating to now close that up—to categorize it as taken to "completion" so that I now have new energy freed up for wonderful opportunities in my life. The space for new focus. I'm exhausted so I'll finish writing tomorrow...

SIGNING THE DIVORCE PAPERS and getting the judge's seal of approval is certainly one aspect of releasing. In fact, it's a hallmark moment in releasing. It's a formality that signifies that you have let go from a life you once knew.

Embrace the concept of letting go of that which no longer serves your highest good.

Thoughts, things, relationships, outdated dreams. Leave the past in the past, right where it belongs. As mythologist, Joseph Campbell, said, *"We must be willing to get rid of the life we've planned, so as to have the life that is waiting for us."*

Commit to leaving the past in the past. Don't turn back. Only move forward. One step at a time. Sometimes, one small baby step at a time.

Tears

If there's one constant to every stage in a divorce, it's tears. Anyone who has traveled through the phases of divorce has shed tears, in one way or another—tears of frustration, anger, denial, grief, and maybe even eventually, tears of joy. Tears are a release of emotion from your body. Tears bring release.

With the extraordinary amount of pain at the dissolution of my marriage, I think I cried a thousand rivers. I cried to my mother and father. I cried to my sister. I cried to my friend. I cried to my pastor. I cried to my therapist. Wow, did I cry a lot, to the point that I thought, "Who is this woman crying and crying and crying?" I'll tell you who that woman was. This was a woman who loved her husband immensely. This was a woman who for 21 years spent her life with a man that she met in high school - her high school sweetheart. This is the one whom she imagined growing old with—meaning the rest of our lives together. There was nothing else that I ever imagined because I loved him deeply and we had something so great.

I imagined us growing old together. I imagined us watching our hands grow old together as we would hold on to one another on long walks or swinging on the porch swing. This is the man who was the father to my dear children. I cried for many things. Why couldn't I just release it and let go? Looking back, I can see that each and every tear was a part of the release.

Letting go

Throughout the divorce process, I hurt so badly that I thought, "How will I ever trust someone again? How will I trust someone and give my love completely if they can possibly just let go and turn around and be gone?' After 21 years, it's crazy. I needed to learn to let go. About the tears, those tears flowed and flowed and flowed. Why? Because they needed to…because that was an accumulation of 21 years of commitment.

Those tears were releasing and unwinding that bond. Because I allowed myself to fully go into the feeling, I was able to let go and heal. You have to feel it and deal with it so you can truly heal it and move on. And you have to let go of destructive thoughts, such as, "I'll never trust anyone again."

How about you?

How have you approached the process of letting go, and releasing what's bottled up inside of you?

The Stupid File

While getting my hair cut, my stylist who is divorced, shared that she had created a "stupid" file for her ex husband. Whenever he does something "stupid" that upsets her and could potentially drive her crazy if she let it, she instead writes it down on a piece of paper and sticks it in the "stupid" file. I laughed so hard at this. It's brilliant. By writing it down and sticking it into a file, she's able to let it go instead of carrying it around in her mind. And on the backside, if she were to ever need this information in the future, it's documented. You could also call this file the "not so conscious" file, "not so smart" file, "complete ass" file, or the "I love you for your strengths and these are not" file. Create a file name that resonates for you. You could also use a box in the event that a file would be much too small of a space. Maybe a storage unit would be more fitting. Not sure.

The Cleanse—Letting Go of "Things"

It feels amazing to let go. It feels liberating to

simplify and let go of the "stuff," the material items. This could be the extra stuff that you no longer need because you've "right-sized" to a smaller living space or this could be items that hold energy or memories that you don't need to carry around with you. I let go of a lot of items that held the energy of the marriage which lightened the load for me both literally and figuratively.

I started out by walking through the house—taking photos down. The first one to come down was a picture of our wedding day. A few days later, I was able to take down another picture, this one from the mantle, a picture of the family, happy on a vacation in Hawaii. Next, I cleaned up my Facebook, deleting outdated photos of us as a couple. I left one of the four of us as a family up. The process continued. Eventually I replaced the old with new photos of the three of us, with new happy memories.

I sold the marital bed.

Then, I took my wedding dress down from a shelf high in my closet, opened the box and looked at it one last time. It was beautiful. I thought about the happy memories of that day, honored it, blessed it for someone else, and donated it.

The box of memories came next—all the cards, souvenirs, love letters, and pictures. I opened the box with my best friend. A well of emotions emerged as I looked through the memories. I picked out a few favorites, closed the lid and left the rest for my ex. *Let go.*

When I was moving, I sold, donated, or gave away more items. I didn't want to "carry" with me the dishes from our wedding, the silverware, the glassware, etc. I let it go. I didn't want the energy or the memories to be in my constant everyday use and place. This also made for a much easier move.

Fire

I had heard about the power of 'releasing the past' by placing an item that symbolizes what you need to release into a fire. Author Debbie Ford spoke of this often as a powerful healing technique for letting go.

I knew I needed to do it because of the power of releasing that comes with going through this formality. I knew I had to let go because the pain of holding on to all of the feelings and memories was too much and was no longer productive. And I knew I wanted to do it before the clock struck midnight and we entered into a new year. I needed to let it go as a part of "last year," giving it more of an "in the past" feeling.

So on New Year's Eve, after my kids were in bed, I released a picture of my ex and me by placing it into the fire.

It was my favorite picture of the two of us—we

were happy and in love. It was from a special night out on a previous anniversary, a night on the town at a jazzy supper club where he had dedicated a song to me. I held it in my hand and had a flash of memories come through my mind and a surge of emotions flood through my body.

It was difficult but I knew I needed to let go.

I knelt down, looked at the picture, took it all in, and then handed it to the fire. With a gulp in my throat, said, "I loved you so much. Thank you," and I let go. I watched it melt, then burn. I watched it get engulfed by flames and melt into the wood and eventually disappear.

I then lit a candle for me, letting go of the concept of two and embracing the concept of oneness. *The light of the candle represented hope and a bright future.*

The Letter

No matter what I faced during my own journey, writing always helped. I wrote countless letters, thoughts, and journal entries. Some I kept to myself, but others I sent. The following letter was written to my ex one full year before I decided to give it to him.

> Dear Kelly,
> I am sitting in the very hotel on Shelter Island that you and I stayed at 10 years ago. I'm writing to tell you how sorry I am that our

marriage dissolved. I had such high hopes for us. For our love. I loved you so much. I was mercilessly grateful for our love. I used to think, "How did I get so lucky?"

The demise of our marriage and the course of the unraveling proved to be my greatest despair. I don't know if I'll ever fully understand why this happened. But I do understand this. We were meant to be married. We were meant to come together for the time that we did. At this moment, tears are dripping off my cheek onto my arm. There's another one, dripping off my nose.

Recently someone asked me how long we were married. When I answered 14 years, the response was, "Wow, you had a good run!" Like it was an accomplishment...And so it was. Even though it didn't last, it was an accomplishment, for it served us tremendously at one time. We had some incredible times together and countless gifts arose from our union, so let's cherish those.

There's no doubt that I hated the hurtful things you've done and said to me. And I know you do, too. I sincerely forgive you. So if you find you are holding onto blame and shame, let it go. If you're carrying guilt, let it go. Evidently, this was part of a grander plan. I forgive you.

I think what's important is that we honor what was, and even more importantly that we honor one another as we move forward. No more nasty, only love. For it is out of love that our children came into this world and our children are our connection.

I wish you the best.

Love & Light,

Lori

Exercise

Take the time to write one letter to yourself of honor and gratitude, and one to your ex of forgiveness, grief, and whatever needs to be said. If you're feeling guilt, write an apology letter. Whether or not you ever give it to your ex, take the time to write it. It's a deeply healing exercise.

The Spiritual Divorce Ceremony

I had a profound experience in healing from divorce. Although many processes helped along the way, nothing freed me the way the Spiritual Divorce ceremony did. It provided a cleansing and release like no other. The releasing of the vows was the most profound turning point in my healing and letting go, and it happened in a day.

When I became married I made a commitment, a vow before God, and I took it very seriously. Now that I was getting divorced, it not only felt natural, but imperative, to address this with God, fully and formally, like we do with the courts, the state, and the lawyers. So much emphasis is put on the legal aspect of the divorce but when I became married, I signed an official marriage license AND took a marital vow—a promise before God. The latter being the most important to me. I didn't want to only clear it through the courts—I wanted to clear it with God.

I share the details of this story and a script of the actual Divorce Ceremony in Chapter Nine, Releasing of the Bonds ~ The Spiritual Divorce Ceremony.

Forgiveness

Forgiveness is incredibly powerful. It's transformative.

Time and time again when I talk to people who have been through divorce I ask, "What was the turning point in your healing?" Time and time again I hear, "It's when I forgave. It's when I offered full forgiveness. Not forgiveness for only some of the things but when I forgave completely. Forgiving your ex for the things they said, things they did, the behaviors they chose. All of it."

You may have been the one who was left behind in the marriage and you wanted it to thrive and last forever. Or you may have been the one who chose to leave. Either way, forgiveness provides a turning point.

Both medical and spiritual texts teach us that by holding onto resentment toward someone or carrying bitterness in your heart, we are literally damaging our physical health and stunting our joy. It can create issues in our tissues.

What does it mean to truly forgive?

Forgiveness means to let go of blame and resentment.

It's a personal choice within yourself to deliberately and consciously choose to forgive.

The personal choice to activate and cultivate forgiveness is where the power lies. It's within you.

There are countless benefits that come with forgiveness.

Forgiveness might not feel natural at first. You may feel very angry. You may feel sad. And it's okay to feel that way. Experience those feelings. It's imperative that you not deny them. And even with those intense feelings, you can begin to forgive. The process all begins by first having a willingness to forgive. With the stack of evidence of how beneficial it is for you to forgive, I'm guessing that you could conjure up a thread of willingness in your heart and mind.

Be willing. Even if you feel this concept is crazy, just try it. Humor me. Humor yourself. Repeat. With time it will happen. And holy man, watch out. You will feel so good, so free. Burdens will be lifted. Did I mention, repeat? Do it again and again, as needed.

What happens during the process of forgiveness? A new level of happiness, strength, and joy emerges. Be willing.

One gentleman shared how during the divorce he was utterly distraught. He was yearning for peace and had a sense of unease. He felt anxious. He felt angry. He could barely sleep. He shared that forgiveness was the turning point for him. Total forgiveness. Not just for some things but for all things that occurred with his ex. He met with his ex and he told her, "I have been feeling a lot of anger toward you and have quite frankly even wished horrible things for you. I don't want to do that anymore. I completely forgive you." From that forgiveness, a strong release and relief for both of them occurred, ultimately gifting the whole family moving forward. It was the turning point in his healing. He immediately began to feel peace and a positive shift in his life as a result. Freedom.

Your ex may have truly done you harm. Forgiving them doesn't make what they chose to do okay. It does not condone their behavior or the effects of it. Forgiveness sets you free. Listen, you never even have to tell them you have forgiven them. It's great if you want to and if it feels right, but it's not a requirement in order for you to receive the immeasurable benefits of forgiveness. Forgiveness is that powerful.

What happens if you choose not to forgive? If you decide instead to hold onto bitter resentment?

If you choose not to forgive, it's as though a film or residue keeps you from shining. And it adds a dimness to your life. If you do not forgive, it keeps you stuck, so tied to the past that it doesn't allow for the present and future to truly open up to its greatness. It holds you back from loving again, from living a joyful life, from living fully.

It's like an energetic hook. If you do not forgive, you ultimately suffer. You can be angry. Own it. Feel it. Let it out. Then forgive.

What if you don't feel like forgiving just yet? What if your spouse has really done harm to you? The answer is you do it to set yourself free.

You deserve to be happy. You deserve to have the freedom of your heart.

When it comes to forgiveness you've got to be ready for it. That means you have to have already let go of the anger, or most of it, anyway. What happens if you do not let go of anger and try to forgive first? Most likely you'll find yourself experiencing repression or denial. So let go of that anger. Kick it out, scream it out, write it out in a journal, or talk to your best friend, your mom, your sister, your therapist. Really work through the anger. Because trying to forgive when you still have the anger is just more of 'stuffing it down' and it will still be there later. So feel the anger when it happens. Allow yourself to feel it when it arises. Then, allow yourself to have grace and let grace fall upon you and forgive.

Forgive the acts of the other person no matter how horrible they have been. You may have to do this again and again and again, as in my case. I have forgiven many times. And even years later I still get the "opportunity" to forgive some more. What about future misgivings or repeated misgivings? Forgive. When you forgive, you keep your personal power. When you give in to unforgiveness, you give your power away to that person.

When the Bible says to forgive not just seven times but to forgive 7×70 times, I often wonder, "I think I've already met that number, so now what do I do?" What I've been choosing to do is to continue to forgive because when we forgive others we're ultimately giving ourselves a gift by letting it go and not carrying the burden. Challenging as it can be sometimes, I know that by choosing to forgive, I'm setting myself free. I decided I am not going to let him have the power to keep me angry or upset. I realize that in the big picture, every time we forgive we create better boundaries. Forgive and keep moving forward with Grace.

Perhaps you feel like you need to be forgiven by your ex in order to really move forward. No one holds that power over you. All you need to do is forgive yourself. Forgiveness releases shame and guilt. God's forgiven you—have you forgiven you? Take your lessons learned and move on. It's not going to do you any good to beat yourself up. Let it go—you've done everything you can do. Let it go and move on. Allow God's grace to heal you.

Forgiveness is a process that sometimes feels unending. Sometimes it takes time to truly forgive. Be gentle and patient with yourself. But once you do forgive, you feel freedom. It's liberating. For when blame, shame, guilt, victimhood, and other negative feelings are replaced by forgiveness, you will have naturally begun construction on a new and more refined version of you.

Forgiveness is transformative when you truly forgive yourself and others. As author Louise Hay teaches, "You don't have to condone their behavior. It's just that you let the whole thing go. You separate yourself from the experience. You let go. It's done. It's disappeared." Set yourself free and move on.

Forgiveness Exercise

In the first part of this exercise, list out the words, actions, behaviors you need to forgive for your ex and for yourself in the space provided below. Do not censor yourself. Go for the guttural.

I forgive _____(ex) for: _____

_____

_____

_____

I love and forgive myself for: _____

Forgiving and letting go is the second part of the process. Close your eyes and, in your mind's eye, imagine your ex surrounded by a white light. See him/her through the eyes of grace. Begin to focus on your breath. Breathe in, "I forgive you." Breathe out, "I release you." Breathe in deeply and repeat the mantra three times.

Repeat this as often as you'd like. Try to do it at least once daily for as long as you need to do it. In a short amount of time, you will notice a difference in the way you feel.

~

Leave the past in the past right where it belongs. Look forward. Don't spend your time looking in the rear view mirror, wishing how things should've been or could've been or replaying over and over as to why things happened the way they happened. Rather, accept what is, claim it, and move forward with a fresh slate, a new beginning—a fantastic new exciting beginning for you in your amazing life.

Embrace the concept of letting go of that which no longer serves your highest good. Choose you. Say yes to you and create a wonderful life for yourself.

Finish each day and be done with it. You have done what you could. Some blunders and absurdities have crept in; forget them as soon as you can. Tomorrow is a new day. You shall begin it serenely and with too high a spirit to be encumbered with your old nonsense.

Ralph Waldo Emerson

Exercise:

What is one thing you can do today to move forward in your healing process? _____
_____

_____

_____

_____

_____

_____

_____

Just one step brings you closer to the fullness of healing, to wholeness.

Chapter Six

ALLOWING THE GOOD TO GUSH INTO YOUR LIFE

Journal Entry:
I've now opened my mind and spirit to what my true authentic life path might be. I am aware. I am open. I am grateful for all that is good. There is so much. I love life and appreciate all beauty. God is good—God is great. I am on an amazing life journey now. There's been a lot of pain but also growth and heartfelt peace. I'm grateful for the inner strength, wisdom, calmness, and peace.

A FEW DAYS AFTER MY DIVORCE, I opened my mailbox to find a Curly Girl Design card from my dear cousin, Jody. The message on the front reads, "She happily set free her heart. After all that—she was surprised to find that she still knew the words to the song in her heart…and she began to sing along." What a sweet and perfect message to receive.

There's so much good waiting for you my friend and you deserve it. Here's the deal…you have to promise that you're not going to get stuck in a rut and therefore not recognize or be available for all the good that shows up in your life. A friend shared this with me once, "The only difference between a rut and a grave are the dimensions."

Once you've successfully released, you open yourself up to a whole realm of possibilities for your life. All is new. All is ready for you.

By releasing the old, you have created a whole new space, a whole new capacity in your mind and in your heart to bring the good in. You've moved out, you've dusted off the old, ready to bring in the next greatness to your life. You've prepared yourself. You've prepared yourself for the next great to be.

This new beginning in your life is a hallmark, a benchmark moment, a rite of passage—for you are moving into a new era. You get to make it great. You get to choose it.

You've been through the fires and now it's time to rise out of the ashes into your greatness. Like the new growth after a forest fire, you will now be more beautiful, glorious, and stronger than ever.

What do you want your new life to look like?

As Dr. Joe Vitale put it so poignantly in the foreword, divorce can mean a new start and a beautiful new life. When I was attending one of his seminars in Austin, Texas, he challenged the crowd to ponder this question, *"How good can you stand it?"* I loved this question. It expanded my thinking. Think about your life from that level of thinking so you can allow the goodness to gush into your life.

Be open

Nothing great leaves my life without something even better replacing it.

Niurka, *Supreme Influence*

Be open. Be ready for all the good that is ready to come into your life. Be aware. Notice the synchronicities all around you. Notice the good things that are happening. Notice the opportunities.

The sad truth is that sometimes after a divorce, people get stuck in the idea that they need to suffer for a certain amount of time before they can be happy or fully enjoy life, so much so that they won't even recognize something truly amazing when it's standing right in front of them. Or worse, they may recognize it but not "allow" the good to come in. Be careful not to sabotage yourself or your future by not allowing the good to come in.

A whole lot of goodness is here for you. You deserve it. Give yourself permission to have it. Know that you are worthy of goodness gushing into your life.

The simple act of "giving yourself permission" can

have a profound effect on actually obtaining it. Declare it now for yourself. Say to yourself or out loud, "I deserve and am fully open to receiving greatness into to my life!"

Life isn't about waiting for the storm to pass, it's about learning to dance in the rain.

Anonymous

Now is the time to give yourself permission. Set yourself on the path of deliberate living. Allow yourself to move forward with excited anticipation for what amazement lies ahead in your life.

This is your time, your time to renew, to start again, to create your life by design. Don't ignore the calling inside of you. You came here to create something. It's your birthright to do that.

If ever a time to stretch outside your comfort zone, it is now. You are on new territory, baby. You have a whole new life and choices and freedom. What can feel difficult or scary is simply that when we step outside our comfort zone, we're experiencing something different than what we are familiar with in our lives, in our routines. If you can just get through the tough part, the rewards are so sweet on the other side, as you will become a stronger, more amazing you. Go to the edge.

Think about what you want your new life to look like.

Recently, I was flying out of Phoenix, Arizona, at night. When we were high above the city I was looking out the window admiring the city lights below. As I was looking, a huge ad jumped out and caught my attention—it was a billboard on the entire side of a tall business building, completely lit up. I couldn't believe that I could see this so clearly from so high up in the air, when everything else looked so small. It was a picture of three guys and it looked like a movie ad. I thought, "Wow, if I can see this ad from this high up in the sky, imagine how big these guys are from the view of the street."

This got me thinking about the symbolism of one's "bigger self." What does your bigger self want? Your bigger self—the one who walks through fear and onto the path of your dreams—doesn't doubt itself.

Your bigger, truer self is confident and strong, and doesn't get hindered by petty things or other peoples' judgments. This bigger you thinks big and loves big. Dreams big. Takes big steps even if they seem daunting.

Imagine a bigger, truer you on a giant billboard, and that billboard is your life the way you want it to be—that which your soul desires it to be. What is your coming attraction? Take this moment. Close your eyes, connect to your bigger, truer self, and ask, "How do I want my life to be? How do I want to show up in the world?"

Sit with that.

Throughout the day and over the course of the next few days, you'll find that your vision for your upcoming attraction will become clearer. This will happen because it's in your conscious mind, at the forefront of your mind, and because of this you have an increased sense of awareness to what you truly want. You could be relaxing in the bath, driving carpool, or out on a walk when suddenly you'll likely receive a download of inspiration. It will feel like, "*Kazaam*! There it is!" You'll have a "Yes!" feeling inside yourself. You'll see greater clarity. Details will appear more vividly. Your call to action, your next steps will show up. When this happens, follow your bliss and enjoy the thrill.

If you know that deep down inside you are much bigger than you are showing up as in your life, you can give yourself permission to show up as who you truly are.

The quality of our life is amplified when we step into the power of our true self and go for our passions and dreams.

Life automatically becomes more joyful and more fulfilling—day in and day out.

Sometimes we limit ourselves and feel like we can't have a particular dream. We settle. It doesn't have to be that way. That's simply a trick the mind is telling us. When you connect to the spirit within yourself, you will know that infinite possibilities are available for you. As we know, with God, all things are possible. Trust that. Know that. You are here to reveal your true self and share your innate gifts.

I believe that we are all beings of Greatness. I believe that we are all born with Greatness. It's already there. It's inside of us. We don't need to search for it like it's something "out there." It's right here. It's within you. Your bright light is shining within you. That inner brilliance is your True Self.

Sometimes we don't see our inner brilliance. Why? Because as we grow from our childhood into our adult years, "stuff" happens. You may have experienced a great tragedy or someone may have hurt you. And along the way we can accumulate layers of shame, blame, guilt, resentments, limiting beliefs, sadness, and fear. These elements can begin to cover, or put a shadow on the bright light within you.

Your inner light is still shining, and brilliantly so. You and others just may not see it so well because of the heavy shadow. You just need to peel away the layers to allow it to illuminate. Holding onto these layers is ultimately holding you back. Now it's time to release these layers so that you can unleash your amazing potential. Forgive all that needs to be forgiven. Release the limitations so that you can stand in your Brilliance.

Know that whatever you are currently facing or whatever you've faced in the past cannot keep you from living an amazing life now. *Don't allow the darkness of yesterday shadow your tomorrows*. Remember, you are not what you have been through—that is an experience of the past. And remember, diamonds are created by intense pressure, so thank those past trials and tragedies. Thank each and every one of them because they helped you grow. They served your highest good. You're about to shine! Make the firm decision today that you are going to go for your dreams. Make the commitment to yourself. You are worthy of it. You deserve it.

When life feels shaky, if you find yourself wobbling off the path of your True Self, *stop*. Breathe. Take a break. Reconnect to your true self. Be gentle with yourself without judgment. Get back on track and stand in your brilliance—grounded in your power.

I remember a time when I was feeling a bit uncertain about things, I went on a walk and repeated in my mind, *"Have faith, have faith, have faith, even though you don't know what lies ahead, have faith, have faith. Rejoice in what's about to come."*

By staying steadfast in your faith, you will know, and you will see the beautiful life emerging before you. It's like a little bud right now and it's expanding and growing, and will be blossoming and flourishing. Soon a whole garden of goodness will be yours. Keep the faith.

Have the courage to be your True Self. *Connect to yourself and boldly go for what you truly want. Allow your vision to become your reality.*

Everything starts to show up when you follow your bliss and live the life your soul intended. It all started for me when I gave myself permission—permission to let go and truly connect to my soul, my True Self. Give yourself permission. Anything you've ever done happened because you first gave yourself permission to do it.

Allow yourself to be who you really are. This is your life. Claim it. Say yes to it.

Give yourself permission to have it. The simple act of giving yourself permission can have a profound effect on actually obtaining it. Declare it now for yourself.

Exercise

Say to yourself or out loud, "I deserve and am fully open to receiving greatness into my life!"

Take a moment and write down this affirmation, or a custom affirmation of your own, that resonates even higher with you. Write it from your heart.

_____

_____

_____

_____

_____

_____

_____

_____

Next, write it on an index card or colorful piece of cardstock and post this card where you will see it regularly. You could also put it in your phone, on your iPad, or on your computer screen.

Live the life your soul intended.

Chapter Seven

CREATE YOUR LIFE BY DESIGN

Journal Entry:

On the day I released my marital vows, Reverend Eileen said, "Imagine that you are sitting with a giant book on your lap and it's opened to the middle with quite a few pages on the left and even more pages on the right. The pages on the left all have writing on them and each page represents a day of your life. The pages on the right are blank except for the very top of the first page because your day has already started so it's already been written on. The rest of the book is up to you to write." She reached out her hand to me as though she was handing me something and said, "You've just been given the pen! Today is the first day of the rest of your life."

THIS IS A FRESH CANVAS and you get to paint the masterpiece that is your life.

What do you want your new life to look like?

Be still and think about what you really want to do during this next chapter of your life. What kind of energy, people, and environment do you really want to be in? Be very clear on the distinction.

At this stage, it's about setting the course to

understand the path and outcome for the rest of your life.

What dreams do you have?

What are your goals?

As you embark on this new phase in life, remember that, "With God All Things Are Possible." *Do not limit yourself. Think big. Do big. Live big. Love big.*

Anything is possible.

Connect to Your True Self

As you begin to create your whole new life by design, it's important that you are in touch with your True Self. When you're connected to your True Self, you feel incredibly alive. It's the connection to the spirit of life at your center—the essence of your true nature. What is your true self? It's the *You of You* at your core—confident, strong, blissful. Connecting to your true self is vital to the human spirit. What does that mean? It means to authentically understand who you are, and what you want out of life. I believe an essential part of living a fulfilling life is discovering who you really are and what you truly want in life. Strive to become aware, and gain clarity.

When you truly know who you are you will experience more joy, peace, and meaning in your life.

Being grounded in who you are gives you the edge of being clear about how you want your life to take shape. It becomes easy to define what kind of relationships you want, the type of career you will have, how you will spend your time, and where you'll direct your energy—in such a way that you will feel incredibly fulfilled.

Sometimes in life, we get so busy "doing"—being busy with the busy-ness of life that we forget who we really are. As parents, spouses, friends, career people, we are always giving of ourselves, naturally. And many times, that's exactly what we want to do and that feels good. When the emphasis shifts however, so that we are no longer making decisions based on what our needs are, we can begin to lose ourselves and slip away from the connectedness to our true self.

It can happen so easily and before you even recognize that it's happening. You can find yourself going down pathways in life that are not fulfilling and lead to unhappiness. That's why it's so important that you remember to take time for you and care for yourself and stay grounded in your true essence. Otherwise, you may end up feeling depleted. Years could go by and suddenly you find yourself standing in the middle of your house asking, "Who am I? I know who everyone else is in my family and what they love, but what do I love for me?"

In other words, get really connected to *you*—take time to connect to that solid place within you—the *who* of who you really are. It takes wisdom to connect to *your* truth, not someone else's truth or expectation for your life.

So many times in life, people will consciously or unconsciously make choices based on what other people will think. Whether it's the car they drive, the job they take, the person they choose to marry, the words they say, the clothes they wear, or something else. But concerning yourself with other people's expectations or trying to seek approval from anyone outside of yourself will not provide you with a fulfilling life. If anything, it diminishes your potential. I have seen this all too often, and, in fact, I used to live it.

Don't give power to the "shoulds" of other people's expectations or plans for you. After all, can anyone else know you better than you? Absolutely not. You know you better than anyone else. Connect to the voice and the vision inside of you. When you are true to yourself, doors open and bliss and opportunity gush into your life.

One of the most powerful ways to connect to your true self is to discover your deepest passions in life. *Connect to your core—to the spirit of life at your center.*

In the workshops that I teach, I take participants through the Passion Test™, which is a powerful step-by-step process that allows people to get crystal clear on their passions, who they really are, and what they really want in life. In this process we step out of our head space where the mind tries to convince us of settling for something less than our soul truly desires, and into the heart space—where true passion arises.

It's so exciting to see the transformation that takes place. Someone can walk into the workshop confused about their life, and walk out of the workshop with their life in their hands. It was through the power of the Passion Test™ that I personally became clear about writing this book.

The creators of the Passion Test™, Chris and Janet Attwood, emphasize the importance of having clarity about what you truly want in life, for clarity is the key for creating anything you want in your life. Janet says, "When you are clear, what you want in your life will show up in your life, and only to the extent that you are clear."

So what do you really love? Ask yourself, "What do I really want?" It's been said that your loves and God's will for you are one and the same. Go deep and ask what does God want you to do? Prayerfully ask and meditate on God's will for you. Be still and listen. What is it that resonates in your heart? What is it that gives you an amazing charge? When do you feel ultra alive? What is it that you are doing when you feel an overwhelming sense of bliss? When do you feel the most connected to your soul? Think about that.

Jump ahead and imagine you are 90 years old sharing your life story with your great-grandchildren. What is it that you want to be able to share with them? What accomplishments? How fully did you live? How big did you love? Now come back to your current age, and plan it.

The first step of this process is to make a list of your deepest passions. Complete the sentence, "When my life is ideal, I am…" When creating this list, it's very important that you're thinking about your "ideal life" and not just your "possible life". Think big. Don't limit yourself and don't concern yourself with the "how." This is about getting clear on the "what." The "how" will show up later as your clarity deepens.

Exercise

When imagining your ideal life, ask yourself, "Where am I? What am I doing? Who am I with? How do I feel?" Then open your eyes and make your list.

When my life is ideal, I am: _____

_____

_____

_____

_____

_____

_____

_____

_____

_____

_____

_____

_____

_____

_____

_____

_____

_____

_____

_____

_____

[For more information regarding the Passion Test™, go to: www.YourAmazingPotential.com]

Create a Vision Board

The process of visualization is important for you in order to recreate a happier picture, a new and transformed image, of your life. Researchers have found that having a vision board is one of the best ways to bring your goals into reality—to create a goal or vision of what your new life looks like.

The vision board exercise is a process of renewal and evolution. Before, there was pain, but on the board, there are photos of hope, life, positive activities, and love. You can create a vision board by collecting images and quotes that symbolize how you want your life to be and pasting those images on a board.

A vision board can be placed centrally in the home for everyone to see, or in a more private space, like your bedroom or closet. Place it somewhere that you'll see it regularly. It's a constant reminder of your new mental space, and new positive outlook on life. It is a reminder of what is and what's to come, versus what was.

My vision board included images that represented successfully writing this book, guiding my children to thrive, connectedness to God, blissful experiences, great health and happiness, a beautiful love, travel, and abundance.

Take the time to create your own personal vision board. It's a fun exercise with a finished product that will make you smile and bring you hope every time you look at it.

Chapter Eight

EVOLVE

> Journal Entry:
>
> As I walked along the old, narrow, cracked-with-character-and-longevity sidewalk leading to the front door of my writing coach's office, church bells began to ring. I paused, looked back toward the sound, and up. And there in the sky, above the roofline of homes and businesses, poised a cross. I grounded my flip-flopped feet into the old sidewalk and the earth beneath. I thought about the meaning of the cross that Pastor Dave shared on Easter Sunday—Love. Hope. Redemption. I smiled, gave praise—full of gratitude for this moment...and for my journey. Life is so magnificent! I am happy and overjoyed and grateful in all the good that is happening. What a glorious day!

EVOLVE: TO CHANGE, to transform, to become something new.

During the toughest part of the divorce, I felt like I was dying. Little did I know I was awakening. *The pain and clean slate that comes with divorce can wake you up to try new things, and think in new ways.* The depths of the pain can open a door for you to try new practices that bring greater peace and evolvement.

I love this quote by Michael Bernard Beckwith, founder of Agape International Spiritual Center, "When you resolve to evolve, your problems begin to dissolve." Isn't that the truth? And it's been said that when a major problem comes our way, we can choose to evolve or we can de-volve. What will you choose?

When something horrible happens in your life you've got a choice. You can become bitter, or better. Bitter is a sad path. If you hold onto bitterness it can burn you from within and create disease and death. How will bitterness benefit your life?

The beauty of awakening is that you can look at the circumstances you've experienced in your past and view it from the gifts you received during that time. What were the golden gifts you experienced in your marriage? For me, it was an amazing love and two beautiful children. Some people I have worked with have said that their gift was getting real clarity about life.

One man I know said that it humbled him, brought him to his knees, and made him draw closer to God.

Remember, as long as you live in the past you can't move forward. Evolving is about forgiveness.

Honoring the relationship and having the awareness for the roles each one of you played is important.

Each person is a gift in our lives. Some people are like angels that have given you certain messages along the way. Others are difficult messengers. They teach you hard things. Love your torturers. They teach you the most valuable lessons.

At one point I decided to make a list of all of the gifts I had received as a result of the divorce. Not literal gifts, but gifts nonetheless. During the pain I wouldn't have been able to recognize them as gifts, but after a lot of healing, I became awakened to the value of those gifts.

How has it blessed you? How has it made you more compassionate? *Look at the situation head on, honestly and fearlessly and ask, "What did I learn from this? How did I grow? What are the blessings that have emerged out of the ashes?"*

As with all people and circumstances, the wisdom we take forth from life experiences bring forth compassion, love, light, and the opportunity, if we choose it, to evolve forward.

When I coach women through the process of becoming all they can be, I tell them, "Take inspired action towards the new goals for your life." Evolving is an evolution. Be still. Take time. But evolve and move forward to your new life. Take positive steps even if they're tiny baby steps. Do something with your kids. Get a new place, buy a new house, or if you can't, then go out and buy paint and get new paint on the walls—especially if you're staying in the same house. Let go of any unhappy feelings or bitter resentment. Forgive and let go.

Life is brighter now in my own journey, and there's a lightness about everything I do. Now when I'm with my boys, I appreciate the alone times. Instead of visualizing a picture where dad is missing, I visualize the reality of a happy joyful existence. I feel stronger now and I have a lot of hope for the future.

I no longer fear life and my ex doesn't have an effect on me like he used to because my boundaries are better. Instead of saying, "Yes, I'll meet you for lunch," and getting sucked into the negative mindset or words he used to throw at me, I keep our communication limited and guarded. We do this through email and text for the most part. Email is a good method of communication.

In the past I met with him face to face, and often it ended in some sort of emotional trauma that would stay with me for days. But now I've put my boundaries tight and don't allow that anymore. I remain detached, while wishing him the best. I'm at peace and, even as

I write this, I'm blessing him with positive thoughts and prayers. I want abundance for him and for me.

I've evolved through my life experience of divorce miraculously, through dark valleys and joyful awakenings. And you will too. Perhaps you've already come out on the other side of it, or, you may be standing on the edge of it, but you will come out of this as a better and more evolved you.

Pain certainly wakes you up and shocks your body into making a mental change. Once the divorce is finalized, it's a clean slate to move on and it's incredibly freeing. Although you've been through pain, now is the time to live in the now. I don't know who said it, but I heard a wonderful quote that sums up the entire process of evolving, *"If you're anxious, you're living in the future, if you're depressed, you're living in the past, and if you're at peace, you're living in the present."*

A peace in your heart brings peace to those around you. And although my journey wasn't always peaceful, I tried my best to maintain it in front of the boys, which is another challenge in the healing process if you've got children. Healing is hard enough when there's no one watching.

Nothing has awakened my heart as much as the pain of a broken family. Nothing has given me as much strength as the time I spent alone in the ruined aftermath of a marriage.

Elizabeth Lesser, *Broken Open*

On Thanksgiving this year, now that the peace is real, and the dust has settled, I woke up thankful for my life and with a peace in my heart. Peace. Ah, how nice to enjoy life again and get on the other side of pain. Peace is a change in perspective. A letting go.

On Thanksgiving we went downtown to feed the homeless, and my boys were so excited to do that and give back. Giving back takes your mind off yourself. My parents were there and we came home and made a traditional thanksgiving feast. There was so much to be grateful for.

At home this year the boys were joyful and we played games, laughed, and my youngest son put on a magic show for grandma and grandpa. Across town, my ex was on his own and texted me, "Happy Thanksgiving." I kept it simple. I texted him back. I didn't get drawn into the drama of what used to be or create any dramatic picture of loss in my head. Loss is real, for sure, but the reality becomes what we create.

This year, like all others, there was a little sliver of loss. I didn't dwell on it, but there was a twinge of sadness. Not for the loss of him, but for the loss of the family unit as a whole, and the idea of what we all used to be. My sister, Vicki, warned me early on during the divorce about how rough holidays would be. She had been through divorce and wanted me to be aware that it would still come up from time to time. It's not out of the ordinary. It doesn't mean you're holding on too hard, or too long. All it means is that you have a trigger of memories past. Acknowledge it and let it go.

I like telling people to meditate; gather all the love in the world, and send it mentally to your ex. Of course, when I said that to one girlfriend she said she'd rather send dynamite! The point is that if you feel love and know what it is, how can you be angry? Don't rush into another relationship to cover up the pain. Date yourself first. You're the most important relationship in your life next to God. And if you do actually go on and date, don't make sacrifices. Get clear on what you really want.

In the movie, *Eat, Pray, Love*, a character said, *"Send him love and light every time you think of him and then drop it."*

Keep moving. That's right. Drop it.

Take time to write out 10 characteristics that you appreciate about your ex. Make a list of them. When you think about your ex, focus on these characteristics and send unconditional love. Also, make a list of 10 characteristics that you love and appreciate about yourself.

Now is the time to go on and do what you have to do.

When I got a spiritual divorce, the pastor emphasized how my husband and I had come together for a reason and now it was time to bless that and move on. I couldn't see it entirely then, but I can now. It takes movement to move on.

Momentum...Evolve

Evolution is about moving forward to a higher level of who you are.

Whether you're aware of it or not, we are always evolving. Sometimes major events in our lives like divorce create quantum leaps in our personal evolution, catapulting us quickly.

Transformation often happens during life's greatest moments of despair.

Where are you now?

True evolution is arriving at that place where you absolutely can look back and know that you've grown, learned, achieved more, become better, and have risen or elected to that next level. At this stage, you've evolved. And no matter who you are, what you're currently going through, or where you've been, you have the ability to teach others and mentor them to get through their own personal tragedies. Use your own personal story to change a life. The life you change might change generations of lives.

From the hard times you went through, you got refined but not refused. The stripes on your back will help heal others. Your wounds will not be wasted.

Meditation, healing, and enlightenment are all good things for your soul. I had heard countless times how meditation is such a wonderful practice that brings great peace into one's life. I'd dabbled with a book, a CD, and a workshop about meditation, but I had never completely taken the plunge into a committed daily practice. One of the most powerful tools I've learned on this journey is Transcendental Meditation.

Transcendental Meditation (TM)

I first heard about the Transcendental Meditation Program™ (also known as TM) in 2007 when I was training to become a Passion Test™ Facilitator in San Diego, California. A few years later, as I journeyed through Fairfield, Iowa, a Jyotish reader said to me, "You've got to learn TM!" He went on to explain that all meditation is about is effortlessly settling down, so that your mind finds its own inner source of pure Being—which has an infinite amount of energy, intelligence, and support of nature. He said, *"Why just dip your toe in it when you can be swimming in that all the time?"*

This sounded pretty compelling to me. I began my search for a TM teacher and found Linda Lasseter in Dallas, Texas, and gave her a call. She invited me to her informational seminar. She said, "You will see results within one week. There will be an effortless flow in your day and you will experience less stress. You'll be able to experience greater potential, intelligence and creativity. You start becoming more you."

Over 350 peer reviewed scientific studies back this technique that is hundreds of years old. She explained that it's not necessary to examine every piece of your past. It's not necessary to analyze your garbage to get rid of it. "You don't have to open up a garbage bag and say, "Oh, there's a tea bag, a paper towel, a banana peel" in order to get rid of it. There's no need to concentrate or contemplate. It's a natural, innocent technique that's very powerful in its ability for people to enjoy life more. It's easy and it works on everyone."

I signed up.

Dear Linda taught me from her home for four consecutive days. She taught me the art of sitting quietly with my eyes closed for 20 minutes twice a day.

I'm loving the practice of TM, and it feels as natural as brushing my teeth now. It's wonderful, grounding, sharpening. I feel like my sense of calm, clarity, acuity, and discernment has risen. Everything she described is true.

Transcendental Meditation invites us to be more fully who we are. It's in our fullness that our true beauty can shine through. It brings you to the fullness of being and opens you up to the beauty around you.

~

The great pain of divorce led me on a healing journey that ultimately helped me evolve into a better me. Now, with the feeling of gratitude, I say, "Thank you, divorce, for the gifts you have provided me and for the eyes to see more clearly."

Chapter Nine

RELEASING OF THE BONDS: THE SPIRITUAL DIVORCE CEREMONY

Journal Entry:

It's the night before my Spiritual Divorce Ceremony at Unity of The Hills Church. I remember journaling the night before my wedding. And here I am journaling the night before my spiritual divorce. There's an energy of anticipation, even an excitement, for this next part of my journey, much like the night before my wedding—yet different of course. There's sadness. I'm excited about the freedom that I will feel once I've released the marriage vows. That releasing will allow me to move on in a more profound way. Really for me, the Spiritual Divorce is much more meaningful than the legal divorce. The legal divorce feels like 'just' a piece of paper—a formality that takes a dreadful wait.

As I shared in Chapter Five, the releasing of the vows was the most profound turning point in my healing and letting go, and it happened in a day.

Although I had felt divorced in mind and body,

accepted it, and even appreciated it in certain ways, there was something more that needed to be released—on a soul level. I felt I needed closure on the last bits and remnants that kept me tied on some level and prevented me from truly 100% moving on.

I embarked on a search to find such a ceremony. I called several churches and no one had ever heard of anything like this. Finally, when I connected to Reverend Eileen at Unity Church of the Hills and shared with her what I was searching for, she responded, "I've never heard of that. I'll search for one and if I don't find one, we'll come up with one." She said she totally understood the power and value of releasing the vows.

I asked my ex to join me. At the time, he wasn't interested. Ideally, I would've liked for him to go through this process of releasing the vows with me. I decided that even though he didn't want to participate, I was going to do this for me.

When I spoke with Eileen, she said she had found a Spiritual Divorce Ceremony, an "unwedding" if you will, in Marianne Williamson's book, *Illuminata—A Return to Prayer*. She pulled liberally from the book, added reverse elements from her Marriage Ceremony, and let Spirit do the rest. It would be a candlelit ceremony representing our eternal Spirit—mine, my ex's, and God's essence. She explained that through the releasing of the vows, I would release him with love and grace for his next adventure and free myself to go on to mine. At the end of the ceremony, we would extinguish the unity candle as a symbol of the releasing of the bond and providing closure.

Wearing the green top which I purchased in Sedona—the spiritual city where I met Linda, the angelic wonder, I pulled up to the church. I parked the car and paused for a moment to take it all in, to amass all that has led me to this moment. To honor where I was at on this journey. To breathe. I felt sorrow. I felt excitement. As I walked along the path to the chapel, I thought, "Today's the day, a new beginning!"

My dearest friend who's seen me through the entire journey from wedding shower and throughout all the phases of my marriage joined me in support, standing by my side like a Matron of Honor. The reverend asked her if she would stand in proxy for my ex and speak the words on his behalf.

We walked into the round chapel off the side of the church. It was a breathtaking, beautiful room surrounded with colorful stain glass windows, each color representing a transformative effect. In the center of the room was the Unity candle, already lit.

When I had talked on the phone with Reverend Eileen Ramsey, she had suggested that I bring my wedding album along to the ceremony. As we looked at the pictures, I said, "He's not the same person." With soft assuredness, she said, "And neither are you."

I set the photo next to the unity candle and the ceremony began.

Divorce Ceremony

This is the releasing of the bond and we do it with love, kindness, and compassion...

We have come here today to share in the spiritual ceremony of dissolution of the union of two people who have decided to walk separate paths. It is right and fitting that we begin this time with a word of prayer.

Loving God, we acknowledge your presence here with us today as these two beloved people begin their new life experiences independent of each other. May each of them always know that You are with them as a source—a source of strength to meet each new challenge, a source of light to walk new paths, and a source of love to fill their hearts anew. Your strength, light, and love shall never fail them now or in any time in the future. And so it is. Amen.

We come together today not in joy but in acceptance. We participate in many ceremonies throughout our lives. Some are filled with awe and wonder, and some are filled with sadness and grief. Yet all rites of passage transitions from one state of being to another—a state of transition for us all.

Today, we are participating in the rite of passage from a state of union to a state of separation. We endeavor to make this passage as gentle as possible without denying the pain that each of you may be feeling. You have taken legal steps to divide into independent persons. Now you are ready to walk the paths that each of you have carved out and you pave a way to a free standing relationship that can have very special qualities of respect and communication. Each of you is ready to find a new sense of purpose that is truly your own. But in order to do that successfully, it is necessary to begin the process of releasing the past—old hurts, fears, and frustrations - and negative thoughts and emotions that might block your way.

In the sixth chapter of Luke Jesus taught us, "Judge not and you will not be judged. Condemn not and you will not be condemned. Forgive and you will be forgiven," and so today we affirm our forgiveness. You let go of the past. We seek to release fear, doubt and guilt. And fill the time that is left in our lives with compassion. We wish for each of you and desire for you only good and the highest and best for all concerned. We join with you in God's presence as you hereby let go of the bond of marriage between you. We ask God's blessing on you as you both seek forgiveness and understanding.

We join with you in the recognition that through grace

and the grace of God, there are no endings but only a chance for new beginnings. And we pray this day for God to give you this new beginning. We pray that this beginning is also blooming for your children.

Okay now if each of you will please light a taper from the family candle and that as you do so, this act symbolizes that although you now lead separate lives, the fire at the centers of your Beings were blended by God and will remain there forever.

(Here we lit our individual candles from the unity candle.)

Certain bonds remain between you. These ties call forth your wisdom and goodness. Let God's guidance lead you always in every act, every thought, and every deed with your interaction with each other.

Now if you'll repeat after me:

I, Lori, hereby affirm my place in the ending of our marriage. Now I enter into a new relationship with you. Please forgive me, I forgive you.

This is where I totally lost it. Tears emerged. It was hard to speak...

I treasure the beautiful things we have shared. I desire only good for you and our children. Above all, I promise to respect you as an individual. I bless you and release you. This is my pledge to you.

Then she asked Leslie, "Can you stand in proxy for

Kelly?" and Leslie repeated the words after Reverend Eileen:

I, Kelly, hereby affirm my place in the ending of our marriage. Now I enter into a new relationship with you. Please forgive me, I forgive you.

I treasure the beautiful things we have shared. I desire only good for you and our children. Above all, I promise to respect you as an individual. I bless you and release you. This is my pledge to you.

Let us pray.

May all that is noble, lovely, and true, all that is enriching and creative, all that is beautiful, be in your lives and abide in your homes forever. May the Light of God surround you and your children. May the love of God enfold you. May the power of God protect you. May the presence of God watch over you all the days of your life. Wherever you are, know that God is and all will be well. Amen.

When everything was complete, we hugged, cried, smiled, and laughed. Another pastor walked in to take a picture of us. She pointed out and marveled at the fact that green, the color of the top I was wearing, represented the transformative effect of "Divine order and renewal".

After the ceremony, Leslie and I walked outside and sat on a bench among the flowers. We just sat for a moment. I felt deep relief and a sense of bliss. I felt free!

> Jounal Entry (two weeks after the Spiritual Divorce):
>
> So much healing has taken place. The spiritual divorce made such a difference for me. Releasing the vows and honoring our own individual paths on the journey of life created a quantum leap shift for healing—releasing—closure. I feel relief and peace. I feel lighter. I feel "here and forward." I'm excited and open to what lies ahead, on all levels.

Chapter Ten

LOOKING ONWARD

Journal Entry:

Oh how I love this moment. Nicolas, Lukas, and I are at the Lakeway Park. We have a Whole Foods bag full of picnic goodies and footballs ready to be passed. Nicolas and Lukas are playing on the swing and I am sitting on my favorite rock spot near the water's edge, wrapped up in the picnic blanket feeling a gentle breeze and sounds of the water lapping and ducks calling. As I look over at my sweet boys, I see two beautiful children, loving brothers—Lukas pushing his older brother now. As I witness their joy, my heart sings. Smiley faces, happy hearts. Lukas just came running over to our familiar spot and asked, "Is today the perfect day for the skipping of rocks?!" "Yes!" I said. And Lukas started collecting perfect skipping rocks. We now have a pile and it's time to start skipping!

YOU MAY ASK YOURSELF, "What do I do from here? What are my next steps?"

As you journey onward, take comfort in knowing that all is well. Every experience you've had has served your highest good.

Trust your intuition as your guide every step of the way in your life. It's a powerful gift that is there to guide you.

And if you don't yet trust yourself or still feel off center, lean on others for support. Ask God. Have plenty of positive people in your corner for advice. Make sure you've got a strong support system and go to them for counsel.

Live life to the fullest!

Never settle for less than you deserve and only you know what that is for you. Only you can define that. It's individually unique for each person.

When things feel crazy, when chaos sets in, breathe. Sometimes there's nothing better you can do in a particular moment than to just breathe. Pause. Take three deep breaths and you'll notice the physiology of your body change. A greater calmness will set in, which helps you stay centered. When things feel overwhelming just relax, do something on your comfort list that we identified earlier in the book. This list is a great go-to in order to de-stress and recalibrate.

Most of all, take one day at a time. Don't try to envision ten years down the road but only this day. Stay in the moment. Stay in this day.

Don't waste time looking in the rear view mirror— and believe that all things are possible. What's ahead of you is better than what's behind you. *Love yourself fully.* It's in loving yourself that you can truly be happy. Loving yourself, you are available to love someone else fully—and to be loved fully by another.

Keep in mind that you are free to date without a plan. Live in the moment.

> *Be present in each situation, without having the need or attachment to have to figure everything out for the future. Live in the now—that's where life is.*

When you find yourself freaking out about needing to know what's next in your life, reel yourself back in. Live in the moment. Focus on right here, right now.

Future Relationships

> *A successful remarriage depends on a successful divorce from the old marriage and the successful emergence of self.*
>
> Abigail Trafford, *Crazy Time*

The word *marry* can seem so big and heavy. The concept, post-divorce, used to scare me. I didn't know if I'd ever want to actually marry again. That would mean that I'd have to trust someone again with my heart, trust that I'd be cared for and treasured. That concept, at one time, didn't seem feasible after having my heart crushed to a thousand pieces by a man I once trusted completely. I feel whole again. All the little pieces are rebuilt and have created a better, stronger, wiser, and lovelier me.

Be aware as you move into a future relationship that you always stay connected to your true self. My therapist recommended that I read the book, *Calling in the One*, by Katherine Woodward Thomas. I did and I highly recommend it. The author takes you through a journey that focuses on internal change that brings you to an ideal emotional state to "call in" the quality of love that you seek.

Believe in love again.

Make this next chapter of your life riveting. Celebrate life—have a "New Beginnings" Party!

Return to this book as often as you need as a place of solace. And when you feel like you're ready, pay it forward. Pass it on. Help a friend. Now you get to light the path for someone else and share your story of healing.

Go forward with your head held high, your heart light, and your spirit boundlessly radiant!

Acknowledgements

First, I want to give a special thanks to my friend and mentor, Joe Vitale, for his continual encouragement and guidance for this journey.

Thank you to the team of coaches and editors—Tammy Kling, Tony Jeary, Saundra Goldman, Mathes Jones, and Jody Peterson Lodge—who helped me put vision, organization, and structure to this book.

To my parents, Arden and Bev Anderson, thank you for always believing in me. To my dear children, Nicolas and Lukas, my shining lights!

To Chris and Janet Attwood for being the positive example and proof that grace can and does exist after divorce.

There's a long list of people who have uplifted or influenced me throughout the process of writing this book, including Dr. Lynn Lawrence, Cyndi Hughes, Jenny Cox, Pastor David Sunde, Linda Lasseter, Adrienne Pelton, Leslie Hubacher, Amity Carriere, Karen Kelliher, my sister Vicki, my brother Brian, Dale Capener, and countless friends and family.

Most of all, I want to thank God for guiding me throughout this process and giving me the words to put onto paper.

I am grateful to all.

About the Author

LORI ANDERSON IS A DYNAMIC and compassionate inspirational coach, writer and speaker. It is her passion to help people connect to their True Self and unleash their amazing potential. As the founder of Your Amazing Potential, Lori is dedicated to sharing her message through writing and her many workshops, coaching sessions, speaking engagements, television and radio shows.

With a background in psychology, Lori has dedicated more than 20 years of her life to the art and science of personal development, human potential, and spirituality. As a Certified Passion Test Facilitator, her workshops specialize in guiding participants to connect to their deepest passions and live the life their soul intended.

In her coaching program, Lori guides people through the transition of divorce and facilitates them in creating an amazing new beginning for their life. This program is based on the concepts in the book, *Divorce with Grace*: grace with yourself, grace with your ex, and grace with the situation. Assimilation of these Graces through the five step G.R.A.C.E. process will empower readers and participants to transcend any remnants of victimhood or bitterness and embrace their divorce process as a "Fantastic Evolutionary Experience."

She lives in Austin, TX with her two amazing boys.

FOR MORE INFORMATION ON SEMINARS AND COACHING, PLEASE VISIT:

www.YourAmazingPotential.com

and

www.DivorcewithGracebook.com

Notes

Notes

Notes

Notes

Notes

Notes

Made in the USA
Lexington, KY
19 November 2016